OF ZAMBIA

RORY McDOUGALL
& DEREK SOLOMON

Published by Struik Nature
(an imprint of Penguin Random House South Africa (Pty) Ltd)
Reg. No. 1953/000441/07
The Estuaries No. 4, Oxbow Crescent, Century Avenue,
Century City 7441
PO Box 1144, Cape Town 8000 South Africa

Visit **www.penguinrandomhouse.co.za**
and join the Struik Nature Club for updates,
news, events and special offers.

First published in 2021
1 3 5 7 9 10 8 6 4 2

Publisher: Pippa Parker
Managing editor: Roelien Theron
Editor: Natalie Bell
Designer: Gillian Black
Proofreader: Glynne Newlands

Reproduction by Studio Repro
Printed and bound in China by Toppan Leefung
Packaging and Printing (Dongguan) Co., Ltd

ISBN 978 1 77584 714 4 (Print)
ISBN 978 1 77584 715 1 (ePub)

Front cover: African Fish Eagle (Robert Fowler/Shutterstock.com)
Back cover: top to bottom: Lilian's Lovebird, Rosy-throated Longclaw (Nik Borrow),
Shoebill, Southern Red-billed Hornbill, Half-collared Kingfisher (Chris Krog)
Title page: Southern Carmine Bee-eater (Roy Glasspool)
Contents page: Böhm's Bee-eater

ACKNOWLEDGEMENTS

With many thanks to Sarah Solomon for her invaluable contribution to this project;
and to the photographers who generously shared their images in this publication:
Erle Alsworth-Elvey, Casper Badenhorst, Adrian Bailey, Maans Booysen, Karin
Border, Nik Borrow, Dan Danckwerts, Roy Glasspool, Lee Gutteridge, the late Chris
Krog, Leanne Mackay, Dori McDougall, Stephanie McDougall, Jacquie Paul, Frank
Rijnders, Grant Reed, Ian Salisbury, Janine Scorer, Roddy Smith, Brett Solomon,
Sarah Solomon, Glenda Sparkes, Claire Spottiswoode and Piet Zwanniken.

CONTENTS

BIRDING IN ZAMBIA

Zambia is home to around 782 bird species; however it is often – surprisingly – underrated as a birding destination. This pocket guide describes 425 bird species commonly seen in Zambia, plus several 'specials' for the country. Chaplin's Barbet and Black-cheeked Lovebird are the only two species endemic to Zambia, while a third species, White-chested Tinkerbird, if indeed a true species, has only ever been recorded once, in 1964.

Zambia's national parks and Important Bird Areas (IBAs) offer some of the best bird sightings in the country. There are 20 national parks, covering about 30 per cent of the country. Many of these are well known, such as South and North Luangwa, Lower Zambezi, Kafue and Mosi oa Tunya. Lesser-known parks that also offer good birding include Liuwa Plain, Lochinvar, Blue Lagoon, Kasanka and Nyika. The remaining ones are more off the beaten track.

An impressive 42 IBAs have been identified in Zambia. These places are important for habitat protection and species conservation, and are identified using an internationally agreed set of criteria. (A detailed list of IBAs is available on the websites for BirdLife International and Birdwatch Zambia.)

Yellow-billed Storks

National Parks of Zambia

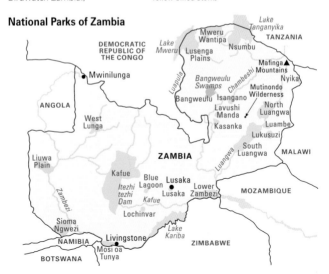

HABITATS AND BIRD DISTRIBUTION

Zambia's habitats are rather complex, reflecting the underlying vegetation zones across the country. This has an influence on bird distribution. Some of the more important habitat types and bird species to be found there are explored below.

Major vegetation zones of Zambia

- Evergreen forests
- *Cryptosepalum* forests
- Afromontane forests
- Miombo woodlands
- Mixed woodlands and mopane woodlands
- *Baikiaea* woodlands
- Grasslands
- Seasonal floodplains, dambos and swamps

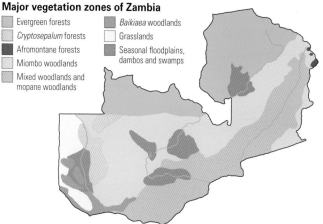

Evergreen forests

This broad and varied habitat includes wet and dry evergreen forest, wet miombo woodland and closed riverine forest.

The northern section of the country is in a higher rainfall zone and the vegetation reflects this with areas of tall, wet, evergreen gallery forests (or 'mushitu' restricted to riverbanks) and wet miombo woodland. The area around Mwinilunga in the northwest is particularly rewarding for birders, with specials including White-spotted Flufftail, Afep Pigeon, White-bellied and Shining-blue kingfishers, Bates's and Bannerman's sunbirds, Honeyguide Greenbul, Laura's Woodland Warbler, Purple-throated Cuckooshrike, Fraser's Rufous Thrush and Spotted Thrush-Babbler. Recent additions to the Zambian list in this habitat include Vermiculated Fishing Owl and Spot-breasted Ibis.

Gallery forests are rewarding for birders looking for specials.

Shining-blue Kingfisher

Roy Glasspool

Dry evergreen forests merge with wet miombo woodlands in the northwest and appear in patches over the rest of northern Zambia; they generally have no surface water. These miombo woodlands are prone to fire, and when burnt they become open-canopy woodlands with a grass understorey, known as 'chipya'. Trees such as *Marquesia*, *Parinari* and *Syzygium* dominate, providing ideal habitat for a whole range of common mixed woodland animals and birds, including Ross's and Schalow's turacos.

Closed riverine, or riparian, forests occur along major and minor rivers, especially the Zambezi, Kafue and Luangwa. In-between the pockets of riverine forest are mosaics of mixed woodland, thickets and termitaria. Target birds include African Pitta, Narina Trogon, African Broadbill, Bocage's Akalat, Grey-olive Greenbul, Livingstone's Flycatcher, Thick-billed Cuckoo and Pel's Fishing Owl. Along the sandy rivers, African Skimmers occur in large numbers together with huge breeding colonies of Southern Carmine Bee-eaters.

Crested Guineafowl – western race

Cryptosepalum forests

Further south and west lies a very important, near-endemic habitat dominated by *Cryptosepalum exfoliatum* subsp. *pseudotaxus* trees. Also known locally as 'mavunda', this almost impenetrable forest is home to the restricted-range Margaret's Batis, Gorgeous Bushshrike, the western race of Crested Guineafowl, and the only ever specimen of White-chested Tinkerbird, collected in 1964.

Cryptosepalum forests, locally called 'mavunda', have a dense understorey and lack surface water.

Afromontane forests

In the extreme northeast are the high-lying afromontane forests of the Nyika Plateau, bordering Malawi. Further north lie the Mafinga Mountains, the headwaters of the Luangwa River. Nyika is currently only accessible via Malawi. At least 40 important bird species are found here and nowhere else in the country. These include Sharpe's Akalat, Fülleborn's Boubou, Churring and Black-lored cisticolas, White-chested Alethe, White-starred Robin, Bar-tailed Trogon and Moustached Tinkerbird.

Afromontane forests have their own unique range of bird species.

Miombo woodlands

More than half of the country is covered by this specialised, deciduous, open woodland. The dominant trees are *Brachystegia*, *Julbernadia* and *Isoberlinia*. Prime miombo destinations include Kafue National Park in the west and Kasanka National Park and Mutinondo Wilderness in the east (just southeast of Lavushi Manda). Mixed bird parties may include Arnott's Chat, Anchieta's Sunbird, African Spotted Creeper, Pale-billed Hornbill, Miombo

Miombo woodlands cover over half of Zambia.

Scrub Robin, Red-capped Crombec, Racket-tailed Roller, Yellow-bellied Hyliota, Chestnut-backed Sparrow Weaver, Bar-winged Weaver and Wood Pipit.

Mixed woodlands

Mixed woodlands are classified by the notable absence of true miombo species and mopane. Key tree species are *Combretum* and *Terminalia*, with some *Acacia* species on the poorer soils. In parts of the Central and Southern provinces, the endemic Chaplin's Barbet occurs in open savanna-type grasslands interspersed with groups of trees containing sycamore figs *(Ficus sycamorus)*. Where thorny *Acacia* species are dominant, this is termed 'munga' woodland. Typical bird species include various doves, Black-collared Barbet, Yellow-fronted Canary, Southern Black Flycatcher, Lilac-breasted Roller, Striped Kingfisher, Fiery-necked Nightjar and Black-headed Oriole.

Mixed woodlands occur in the southeast.

Mopane woodlands, with their sparse grass undercover, host a varied avifauna.

Mopane woodlands

Mopane (*Colophospermum mopane*) woodlands occur on the alluvial clays found in the Luangwa and Lower Zambezi valleys. They are interspersed with baobabs and often with termitaria, covered by thicket. Three-banded Courser, Meves's Starling, Red-headed Weaver and White-browed Sparrow-Weaver are typical species. These woodlands are also home to two species of lovebirds: Lilian's Lovebird and Black-cheeked Lovebird, Zambia's second endemic species, which has a very restricted range in the south only.

Baikiaea woodlands

Pockets of Zambezi teak (*Baikiaea plurijuga*) woodland, with a dense thicket understorey known as 'mutemwa', occur on deep Kalahari sands northwest of Livingstone. This is home to Bradfield's Hornbill, African Hobby and occasionally Shelley's Sunbird, with a smattering of miombo specials where the forest opens up, such as Miombo Tit, Miombo Rock Thrush and Racket-tailed Roller. Here the Acacia Pied Barbet overlaps with Miombo Pied Barbet.

Baikiaea woodlands occur in the southwest.

African Hobby

There are pockets of grasslands throughout the country.

Grasslands

Zambia has large areas of seasonally wet, watershed grasslands; the wetter forms are called dambos. These appear as grasslands in the dry season and as shallow seasonal wetlands when flooded (e.g. northwestern Mwinilunga region). Grimwoods, Fülleborn's and Rosy-throated longclaws, Black-collared Bulbul, Angolan Lark, Black-and-rufous Swallow, Swamp Nightjar, Fawn-breasted Waxbill and Locust Finch occur on the drainage lines. Wet

White-bellied Bustard

season visitors include Blue Quail, Streaky-breasted Flufftail and Great Snipe.

Home to the isolated White-throated Francolin, White-bellied Bustard and Eastern Clapper, Monotonous and Pink-billed larks, grasslands to the west are extensive areas of dry, savanna grasslands on Kalahari sands, including the important seasonal wetlands of Liuwa Plain. Further pockets are dotted throughout the country.

On the high-lying eastern Nyika plateau, afromontane grassland with bracken–briar dominates. These areas are on the fringes of the afromontane forests. Target birds include Blue and Angolan swallows, Hildebrandt's and Red-winged francolins, Cinnamon Bracken Warbler, Scarlet-tufted Sunbird and Marsh Widowbird.

Seasonal floodplains, dambos and swamps

There are wide floodplains along some major rivers and tributaries, such as the upper and lower Zambezi, Kafue, Luangwa and Chambeshi. These provide extensive habitat for Zambia's national bird, the African Fish Eagle, as do the edges of large natural lakes, including Tanganyika and Mweru in the north.

African Fish Eagle

Floodplains are found along Zambia's major rivers.

Floodplains with permanent water and seasonal dambos, shallow wetlands or small grassy floodplains in areas surrounding Lochinvar, Blue Lagoon and Liuwa Plain, provide for large concentrations of waders, waterfowl, rallids, herons, egrets, cormorants, jacanas, terns, ibises, storks and pelicans, alongside specials like Slaty Egret and Wattled Crane.

Large floodplains and dambos sometimes merge into wetland swamps, the most notable being Busanga (in the north of

Slaty Egret

Kafue), Bangweulu and Kasanka. Many provide refuge for moulting waterbirds and suitable habitat for important localised specials like Papyrus Yellow Warbler, restricted to the papyrus swamps of the Luapula mouth, and Shoebill and Katanga Masked Weaver in Banguwelu.

Lochinvar is teeming with birdlife in the wet season.

HOW TO USE THIS BOOK

This pocket-sized book has been designed primarily for use in the field, but if you read it at leisure before you venture out, it will enrich your birding experience. By studying the photographs carefully, you will become more adept at recognising many of the region's birds. For example, if you have looked at the photograph of the Böhm's Bee-eater many times, you may instantly recognise the bird the very first time you encounter it in the field.

Features of each species description

1 **Common name** This guide follows the taxonomy in the International Ornithological Committee's (IOC) World Bird List.

2 **Scientific name**

3 **Length of bird** (from bill tip to outstretched tail). Where a breeding male has a longer tail, the tail length is given separately in the text.

4 A **distribution map** broadly shows where in the region the bird occurs. (**Green** = Resident; **Blue** = Palaearctic migrant; **Orange** = Intra-African migrant)

5 The **description** outlines obvious and diagnostic features to aid quick identification.

6 **Status** conveys the bird's relative abundance within the region: resident, common, vulnerable, endangered, etc.

7 **Habitat** describes the type of vegetation in which the bird occurs and is often an important clue to its identity.

8 **Voice** describes the bird's call – a great aid to identification.

9 **Photographs** have been chosen to show each bird's most obvious features. Where there is a marked difference between sexes, breeding and non-breeding plumages, or between ages – more than one photograph has been included.

34   EAGLES

Lesser Spotted Eagle   *Clanga pomarina*
55–67cm (wingspan 146–168cm)
Sexes similar. Dark brown with a diagnostic rounded crown with no crest, lightly feathered 'stovepipe trouser' legs, and a plain rounded tail. Eye yellow-brown. Similar Wahlberg's Eagle has small crest, brown eye and long, square tail. Juv. has white spots on upperwing coverts, and brown eye. In flight, shows narrow white line between flight feathers and wing coverts, and white crescent on rump. **Status:** Palaearctic migrant, from late October to March. Can be gregarious. **Habitat:** Well-wooded or open country. **Voice:** Silent when in Africa.

Wahlberg's Eagle   *Hieraaetus wahlbergi*
53–61cm (wingspan 130–146cm)
Sexes similar. Small eagle, with variable plumage from dark brown to pale buff. Easily confused with Lesser Spotted Eagle but small crest, baggy leg feathers (not 'stovepipe trousers') and dark brown eye are important distinguishing characteristics. Diagnostic straight-edged wings and narrow, square-ended tail in flight. Juv. resembles adult. **Status:** Common intra-African br. migrant, late July to April. **Habitat:** Any woodland especially miombo. **Voice:** Loud, mournful cry in flight, rapid yipping contact call at the nest.

Tawny Eagle   *Aquila rapax*
60–75cm (wingspan 170–200cm)
Sexes similar. Large eagle with variable plumage, from pale brown through reddish-brown to dark brown. No dark trailing edges to wings (see Steppe Eagle). Eye yellow-brown; yellow gape extends to centre of the eye (see Steppe Eagle). Tail long and rounded in flight. Juv. usually lighter in colour; pale dark brown. **Status:** Common in Luangwa Valley and the south, uncommon in other parts. Occurs singly or in pairs. **Habitat:** Open woodlands and woodland savanna. **Voice:** Short bark when breeding.

Abbreviations used in this book

ad. = adult   **imm.** = immature   **juv.** = juvenile
br. = breeding   **non-br.** = non-breeding   **♂** = Male **♀** = female

GLOSSARY

Alula Small group of feathers growing from wrist joint of wing

Bird party A feeding flock of mixed bird species, possibly for increased foraging efficiency

Brood parasite A bird that lays its eggs in the nest of another species

Call Short notes given for alarm and contact purposes

Casque Horny ridge on the top of the bill of some species e.g. hornbills

Cere Fleshy covering at base of upper beak of some birds e.g. raptors

Chipya Colloquial Zambian for burnt, dry, evergreen forests

Cloudscraping High-flying behaviour

Cooperative breeding Non-breeding flock members assist breeding pair during nesting cycle

Crepuscular Active during twilight (dusk and dawn)

Dambo Seasonal and shallow grassy wetlands

Decurved Curved downwards

Displaying Conspicuous behaviour relating to courtship, territory, alarm, food source etc.

Ecotone Transitional area between two habitats

Endemic A species found only in a specific region

Flush To drive a bird from its cover

Frons Forehead, feathered front of crown

Gape Base of a bird's bill, where the upper and lower mandible meet

Hawk To hunt

Hepatic Red-brown colouring

Immature A bird that has moulted its juvenile plumage but does not yet have adult plumage

Intra-African migrant Species that migrates within Africa

Juvenile A young bird still in its first complete set of feathers

Malar stripe Stripe on cheek

Mavunda Colloquial Zambian for *Cryptosepalum pseudotaxus*-dominated woodland

Midstratum Middle level of trees

Miombo Largest group of deciduous woodland on the Zambian plateau

Morph An alternative plumage colour

Munga Colloquial Zambian for thorny *Acacia* woodland

Mushitu Colloquial Zambian for tall, wet, evergreen gallery forests

Mutemwa Colloquial Zambian for *Baikiaea* (teak) woodland

Near-endemic A species whose range extends only marginally outside the region where it is generally found

On passage Moving to another area

Orbital ring Eye-ring

Palaearctic migrant Long-distance migrant species that breeds in Europe and northern Asia, and winters in sub-Saharan Africa

Parasitise To lay eggs in another bird's nest

Pennant A long, tapering feather

Race A geographic subspecies which has developed unique characteristics but is still genetically similar to the original species

Raptor A bird of prey

Resident Remaining in the same region throughout the year

Rictal Of a bird's beak, where upper and lower mandibles meet

Riparian Of or adjacent to riverbanks

Riverine Of or adjacent to riverbanks

Song A long, often melodious series of notes, usually associated with courtship and territory maintenance

Speculum A patch of often iridescent colour on secondary wing feathers of many duck species

Supercilium Eyebrow

Termitaria Termite mounds

Territory An area that a bird establishes and defends from others

Vent Feathered area from belly to undertail coverts

Vestigial Reduced

Wing-fripping When wings are vibrated vigorously, producing a percussive sound

PARTS OF A BIRD

BODY FEATURES

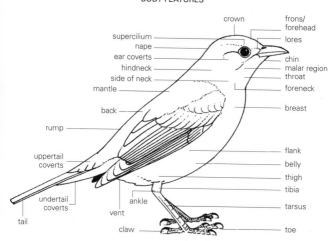

crown
frons/forehead
supercilium
lores
nape
ear coverts
chin
hindneck
malar region
side of neck
throat
mantle
foreneck
back
breast
rump
flank
uppertail coverts
belly
thigh
tibia
undertail coverts
ankle
tarsus
vent
tail
claw
toe

WING FEATURES

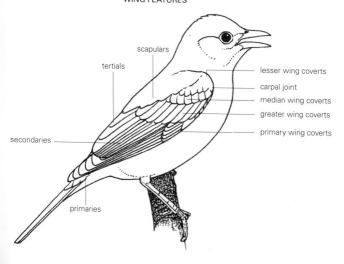

scapulars
tertials
lesser wing coverts
carpal joint
median wing coverts
greater wing coverts
primary wing coverts
secondaries
primaries

White-faced Whistling Duck
Dendrocygna viduata

44–48cm Sexes similar. Distinguished from other ducks by diagnostic white face and throat, the face sometimes stained brown from feeding in muddy water. Lower neck and breast chestnut; belly black. Sides of the breast and flanks barred black and white. Juv. has a brown face and less obvious barring on the flanks. **Status:** Widespread throughout Zambia, mostly in flocks. **Habitat:** A wide variety of wetlands, including floodplains and farm dams. **Voice:** A high-pitched three-note whistle often given in flight.

Spur-winged Goose
Plectropterus gambensis

75–100cm A very large black goose with a white belly, white forewings and a red bill. Male has a partially white face, red facial skin extending behind the eye; red knob on forehead swells when breeding. Female smaller with less facial skin and less white on underparts. Juv. lacks bare facial skin and is browner on the body. **Status:** Common countrywide. **Habitat:** Large floodplains and adjacent grasslands and farmlands. **Voice:** A wheezy two-note whistle.

Knob-billed Duck   *Sarkidiornis melanotos*

64–79cm A large black-and-white duck with a speckled head. Upperparts have metallic sheen. Male has a distinctive fleshy knob on the upper bill that swells when breeding, and shows some yellow on the flanks. Female duller and smaller, and lacks fleshy bill knob. Juv. has buffy brown underparts and dark brown upperparts. Imm. similar to female but heavily barred and speckled on head and neck. **Status:** Common year-round. **Habitat:** Lakes and pools where the water is shallow; flooded grassland. **Voice:** A deep, croaking 'quack' and soft whistles.

Egyptian Goose   *Alopochen aegyptiaca*

63–73cm Sexes similar but female smaller. Large, long-legged, upright buffy-brown duck with black rump and tail and distinctive dark patches on eye and breast. Juv. is duller, only developing eye and breast patch after three to five months. **Status:** Common resident along large rivers such as the Luangwa and Zambezi, and the Kafue Flats. Very vocal and aggressive. **Habitat:** Favours extensive sandbanks on rivers and dams. **Voice:** The female gives a loud, honking call, the male a hoarse hissing, often at night.

African Pygmy Goose   *Nettapus auritus*

27–33cm A tiny duck with metallic-green upperparts, orange breast and flanks, and a white face. Obvious white upperwing patch in flight. Male has lime-green patch, outlined in black, on sides of head and bright yellow bill. Female duller with a lightly mottled face, no green head patch and a brown bill. Juv. similar to female. **Status:** Uncommon resident. In pairs or small family groups; can form large congregations in winter. **Habitat:** Well-vegetated lagoons, particularly amongst *Nymphaea* waterlilies. **Voice:** A soft, two-note twittering whistle.

Hottentot Teal   *Spatula hottentota*

32–36cm Sexes similar but female duller. A small brown duck with a bright blue bill, dark crown, buffy white cheek, black neck patch and dark brown speckling on neck and breast. Green speculum with thin, white, trailing edge obvious in flight. **Status:** Locally common; usually in pairs or small flocks. **Habitat:** Secluded ponds in swamps, lakes and lagoons with shallow water. **Voice:** Harsh chattering call around nest. Female gives a soft 'quack'; male a twittering whistle.

Jacquie Paul

Yellow-billed Duck   *Anas undulata*

51–58cm Sexes similar but female slightly smaller. A large grey-brown duck with diagnostic bright yellow bill with black saddle on upper mandible. Pale fringes to feathers give scaled appearance. In flight, shows green speculum with narrow white border. Juv. less distinctly scaled. **Status:** Common resident in suitable habitat. **Habitat:** Dams, pools in floodplains and slow-moving rivers with pools. **Voice:** A deep quacking call.

Red-billed Teal   *Anas erythrorhyncha*

43–46cm Sexes similar. A medium-sized duck with distinctive dark brown cap, red bill and pale cream-white cheeks. Body greyish-brown but belly lighter; pale edges to feathers give mottled appearance. In flight, secondaries have a broad white edge. Juv. duller with indistinct body mottling. **Status:** Common resident in suitable habitat. **Habitat:** Lakes, dams and floodplains with shallow water. **Voice:** A loud, rather wheezy 'quack' by female; male a soft whistle.

Helmeted Guineafowl   *Numida meleagris*

Claire Spottiswoode

Race *N. m. marungensis*

Race *N. m. mitratus*

55–60cm Sexes similar. A familiar, roundish black bird with extensive white spotting, blue facial skin with red-tipped blue wattles and unfeathered neck. Bony casque in race *N. m. mitratus* is horn-coloured and broader, orange in race *N. m. marungensis*. Juv. brown with white speckles, lacks casque; with striped black and red-brown feathered crown. **Status:** Common throughout Zambia; *N. m. mitratus* in the south and east, *N. m. marungensis* in the north. **Habitat:** Wide variety of woodland habitats; cultivated lands. **Voice:** Variety of raucous, cackling calls; metallic two-note contact call.

Coqui Francolin — *Peliperdix coqui*

20–26cm A small francolin, male with chestnut head and neck, and black-and-white barred breast and belly. Female has white throat and face bordered by black necklace. Legs of both sexes yellow, male with spurs. Juv. resembles female but is paler above, with chestnut mottling below. **Status:** Common resident in much of Zambia. **Habitat:** Wide variety of grassy habitats and woodland – particularly miombo. **Voice:** Two-syllable cackling 'coqui'; male a tinny 'kreek'.

Shelley's Francolin — *Scleroptila shelleyi*

30–35cm Sexes similar. A francolin with white chin and throat, and narrow black necklace; legs are yellow. Race *S. s. whytei* has buff to grey speckled underparts, race *S. s. shelleyi* has clear black speckling on the belly. Similar to female Coqui Francolin, but much larger and with a narrower eye-stripe. **Status:** *S. s. whytei* widespread in west and north, *S. s. shelleyi* restricted to south and southeast. **Habitat:** Open miombo and mopane woodland; prefers rocky and stony areas. **Voice:** A high-pitched four-note call described as 'I'll drink your beer'.

Crested Francolin — *Dendroperdix sephaena*

30–35cm Sexes similar. This francolin has a broad, white eye-stripe and obvious white streaks on back, with black blotches on neck and breast. A raised tail gives a bantam-like appearance. Legs are dull red; female lacks spurs. Juv. resembles adult, but paler. **Status:** Common resident, very territorial. **Habitat:** Thickets and woodlands, often with sparse ground cover, and dry, riverine vegetation in the southern third of the country. **Voice:** Loud, cackling song often preceded by low growls, many times given as a duet.

Natal Spurfowl   *Pternistis natalensis*

30–38cm Sexes similar. This spurfowl has grey-brown upperparts with black feather-shaft streaks, and paler underparts with distinctive vermiculated black-and-white markings. Easily identified by lack of bare skin on face and throat (see Swainson's Spurfowl). Bill and legs are orange; spurs on legs. Juv. paler and greyer with greenish bill. **Status:** Locally common in east and south. **Habitat:** Dense thickets and dry riparian forest. **Voice:** Raucous, screeching call; when disturbed gives a rapid harsh call in flight.

Red-necked Spurfowl   *Pternistis afer*

25–38cm Sexes similar. A spurfowl with diagnostic bright red face, throat, bill and legs. Upperparts are brown with black or brown stripes on feather shafts. Underparts vary significantly, from black and white streaking in eastern race, to rufous-brown streaking in other races. Juv. duller, plumage browner, bill brownish, legs dull red. **Status:** Locally common resident, mostly absent from extreme southwest. **Habitat:** Dense rank grass cover in all types of open woodland, old cultivation, montane grassland and clearings in *Cryptosepalum* forest. **Voice:** Harsh, croaking call.

Swainson's Spurfowl *Pternistis swainsonii*

33–38cm Sexes similar. A dark brown bird with a bare red face and throat, black upper mandible and red lower mandible. Black legs distinguish it from Red-necked Spurfowl. Juv. duller overall, with less red facial skin. **Status:** A common resident in the southern half of the country and up the Luangwa Valley. **Habitat:** Favours tall grassland in a variety of open woodland types; also abandoned cultivated lands, usually close to water. **Voice:** A series of hoarse, grating notes.

Little Grebe (Dabchick)
Tachybaptus ruficollis

25–29cm Sexes similar. A small dark grebe with a grey-black cap, rufous cheeks and neck, and diagnostic pale patch at base of the short, black bill. Eyes are red. Long, fluffy chestnut-coloured feathers on the flanks. Non-br. birds are paler, particularly on the back and neck. Juv. head is streaked, eyes are brown. **Status:** Widespread but uncommon in the northeast, Luangwa and Lower Zambezi. **Habitat:** Lakes, ponds, small farm dams, reservoirs and particularly sewage ponds. **Voice:** A loud, rapid and frequent trill.

Yellow-billed Stork
Mycteria ibis

95–105cm Sexes similar. Br. ad. all-white with pink-washed wings,except for black flight feathers and tail. A large, yellow, slightly decurved bill and bare red skin on face and forehead (orange-red when not breeding) are diagnostic. In flight, the black tail distinguishes it from the White Stork (tail white). **Status:** A common breeding resident, mostly seen in colonies. **Habitat:** Floodplains, lagoons and edges of larger rivers. **Voice:** Generally silent, but bill-clatters when displaying.

African Openbill
Anastomus lamelligerus

80–95cm Sexes similar. All black. Large horn-coloured bill has conspicuous gap in the middle; mandible tips specially designed to extract molluscs and snails from shells. Juv. has white-tipped feathers and a straight bill with no gap. Br. birds have glossy elongated lower neck and mantle feathers. **Status:** Widespread resident with some local movement between colonial breeding and non-br. areas. **Habitat:** Shallows of large floodplains and lagoons. **Voice:** Usually silent. Gives loud, cackling calls at breeding sites.

Abdim's Stork
Ciconia abdimii

75–80cm Sexes similar. Black upperparts, diagnostic white lower back and belly. Bill greenish with red tip, facial skin dull blue with red spot in front of the eye. Legs greenish-grey with red 'knee' joints and feet. Juv. duller and browner. **Status:** Common intra-African non-br. migrant occurring mainly October to April. Highly gregarious. **Habitat:** Floodplains, dambos and grasslands. Feeds in large flocks on agricultural lands during outbreaks of armyworms and locusts. **Voice:** Mainly silent in southern and central Africa.

Woolly-necked Stork
Ciconia episcopus

86–95cm Sexes similar. Black body with purple iridescence. Soft, curly white feathers on neck create a woolly appearance. Belly white, bill black with red tip and red ridge on upper mandible. Juv. duller with no purple iridescence, neck brownish and face blacker. **Status:** Widespread and common in Luangwa Valley and Kafue Flats. Breeds in riparian forest in the north. **Habitat:** Favours open grassland, usually close to water, and edges of rivers and streams. **Voice:** Generally silent.

White Stork
Ciconia ciconia

100–120cm Sexes similar. Large, all white apart from black flight feathers. Bill and legs red, but legs often whitish when covered with excrement. In flight, white tail distinguishes it from Yellow-billed Stork (black tail). Juv. with black bill, red at base, and brownish wing coverts. **Status:** Common Palaearctic migrant recorded mainly in November and December on southwards passage, and late February to April returning northwards. Often in large flocks. Some remain throughout summer. **Habitat:** Open grassland, pasture or floodplain. **Voice:** Silent except on nest.

Saddle-billed Stork
Ephippiorhynchus senegalensis

145–150cm Large black-and-white stork. Diagnostic red-and-black banded bill with bright yellow saddle at base of upper mandible. Long legs have pink-red 'garter' at 'knee' joint. Male has brown eyes and small yellow wattles at bill base. Female has yellow eyes. Juv. head, neck and bill grey with no saddle. **Status:** Sparsely distributed resident. Usually found in pairs. **Habitat:** Larger floodplains and major rivers. **Voice:** Generally silent.

Marabou Stork
Leptoptilos crumenifer

120–150cm Sexes similar. Unmistakable stork with massive bill, unfeathered head and neck, and pendulous inflatable throat pouch; red skin at back of neck. Upperparts slate-grey, underparts white. Grey edges to wing feathers. Juv. head and neck covered with down, wings brownish. **Status:** Locally common. **Habitat:** Open grasslands, lagoons and floodplains. Scavenges around abattoirs and refuse dumps. **Voice:** Goose-like honks, squeals, whistles. Bill-clattering by adults and chicks at nest site.

African Sacred Ibis
Threskiornis aethiopicus

66–84cm Sexes similar. A mainly white ibis with black, unfeathered head and neck. Distinctive heavy, decurved black bill. Fluffy black scapular feathers. When breeding, underwing skin turns pinkish-red and flanks turn buffy-yellow. Juv. has a mostly black-feathered head and neck; imm. neck speckled with white. **Status:** Locally common. Occurs year-round with influx of birds from the south from August to January. **Habitat:** Edges of pans and dams, large rivers and floodplains. **Voice:** Croaks and squeals at nest sites.

Hadada Ibis　　*Bostrychia hagedash*

76–85cm Sexes similar. Grey-brown with an iridescent green sheen on wing coverts. Bill large, dark brown and decurved, with dull red ridge on upper mandible. Narrow white stripe runs from base of bill below the eye. Juv. lacks the green sheen of the adult. **Status:** Widespread resident in limited numbers. Scarce on Kafue Flats and in suburbia. Usually in pairs or small groups. **Habitat:** Well-developed riparian fringing forest along major rivers and lagoons. **Voice:** Loud, distinctive, raucous call, usually given in flight.

Glossy Ibis　　*Plegadis falcinellus*

55–70cm Sexes similar. Slender, long-legged ibis with dark chestnut head, neck and body. Wings, back and tail have metallic, glossy green sheen when breeding. Non-br. birds duller with fine, whitish streaks on head and neck. Bill long, narrow and decurved. **Status:** Generally scarce, but large numbers may occur in Blue Lagoon, Lochinvar and Liuwa Plain in height of rains. **Habitat:** Swamps and floodplains. **Voice:** Usually silent, but harsh croaking sound when breeding.

African Spoonbill　　*Platalea alba*

86–90cm Sexes similar. A distinctly all-white bird with diagnostic long and spoon-shaped bill. The upper mandible is grey with red edge, lower mandible black. Facial skin and legs red. Juv. face feathered; eyes, legs and outer primaries darker. **Status:** Locally common in Liuwa Plains, Kafue Flats and Luangwa Valley when breeding in small colonies. Non-br. birds wander extensively. **Habitat:** Major lakes and river margins. **Voice:** Mainly silent but makes croaking noises and claps bill around nest site.

Dwarf Bittern
Ixobrychus sturmii

25–30cm Sexes similar. Small with slate-blue upperparts and buffy, heavily marked underparts. Broad black streaks on breast and belly. Legs yellow-green, becoming orange pre-br. Eye red-brown. Juv. duller and paler, with mottled upper body feathers with buffy tips. **Status:** Uncommon intra-African br. migrant occurring November to April. Presence dependent on rain. Easily overlooked; skulks or freezes in defence. **Habitat:** Seasonal wetlands with low inundated trees for nesting. **Voice:** Loud croak when disturbed.

imm.

White-backed Night Heron
Gorsachius leuconotus

50–56cm Sexes similar. This bird has a large black head, short crest, large eyes with conspicuous white eye-ring and chestnut neck. Upperparts brown, throat white. Narrow white patch on back normally only seen in flight. Juv. paler brown with heavy brown and white streaking on underparts, and white spots on wings. **Status:** Uncommon resident, easily overlooked. Single or pairs, nocturnal and crepuscular. **Habitat:** Quiet backwaters on larger, well-wooded rivers. **Voice:** Low growls or deep 'chucks'.

Black-crowned Night Heron
Nycticorax nycticorax

55–60cm Sexes similar. A small, stocky heron, with black crown and back; forehead, neck and underparts white; wings grey. Eye crimson; legs pale yellow. Br. birds have long white head plumes (shorter in female) and red legs. Juv. brown with prominent large white spots on back and heavy streaks on underparts. **Status:** Widespread resident. Mainly nocturnal and crepuscular. **Habitat:** Reedbeds and papyrus. **Voice:** Mainly silent. Harsh quacking or growling call when breeding or taking flight.

Striated Heron
Butorides striata

40–44cm Sexes similar. Small with dark grey-green back and wings (back is greener than in Dwarf Bittern and appears more scaled). Crown dark with black erectile crest; bill large, black. Underparts pale grey, throat white. Legs orange when breeding, yellower in non-br. birds. Juv. dark brown above with small white spotting on wings, paler and heavily streaked below; shows distinct crown. **Status:** Mainly solitary, common resident. Known to bait prey. **Habitat:** Streams and rivers, dams and ponds with fringing wooded vegetation. **Voice:** Single, sharp call when flushed.

Squacco Heron
Ardeola ralloides

42–48cm Sexes similar. Small, buffy-brown and white with streaked head and neck. In flight, white wings, tail and underparts are distinctive. Non-br. birds have a greenish-yellow bill, which turns blue when breeding. Juv. dull and browner with white streaks over scapulars. **Status:** Widespread and locally common resident. Skulks and stays motionless for long periods. **Habitat:** Edges of dams, pans and floodplains with extensive floating vegetation. **Voice:** Usually silent but gives harsh squawks, mainly when breeding colonially.

Rufous-bellied Heron
Ardeola rufiventris

38–40cm Sexes similar. Small with dark slate-grey upperparts and rich rufous belly, wings and tail. Dark plumage contrasts with bright yellow feet, legs and facial skin. Upper mandible grey-brown, lower mandible yellow; bill has black tip. Br. male has dull red face and legs. Female duller with pale throat and foreneck. Juv. paler than female, with white streaking on underparts. **Status:** Widespread skulking resident, usually solitary. **Habitat:** Floodplains, inundated dambos, dams, edges of lagoons. **Voice:** Mainly silent, gives a single croak.

Lee Gutteridge

Western Cattle Egret
Bubulcus ibis

48–54cm Sexes similar. Smaller than other white egrets, with short yellow bill and stout, short neck. Br. birds have buff plumes on head, neck and breast. Prior to breeding, the eyes, bill and legs turn red. Juv. bill, legs and feet black. **Status:** Common and widespread, mostly non-br. resident. Gregarious. **Habitat:** Grasslands and floodplains, including extensive farming areas. Regularly found together with wild herbivores and domestic cattle. **Voice:** Various croaking sounds.

non-br.

br.

Grey Heron
Ardea cinerea

90–100cm Sexes similar. Large, pale grey heron. White crown and neck with broad black streak above the eye extending to back of head. Eyes, bill and legs yellow. In flight, distinguished from the Black-headed Heron by all-grey underwings. Juv. body paler grey, forehead and crown grey with white ear coverts and yellowish legs (see juv. Black-headed Heron). **Status:** Common resident in wetland habitats. **Habitat:** Dams, rivers, floodplains and ponds. **Voice:** A single loud croak mainly given in flight.

Andreas Trepte, www.photo-natur.net

Black-headed Heron
Ardea melanocephala

92–96cm Sexes similar. Large greyish heron with black head and hindneck, and white throat. Legs are black and has a black upper mandible and greenish lower mandible. Two-tone underwing pattern shows black flight feathers and grey underwing coverts, distinguishing it from all-grey underwings of Grey Heron. Juv. crown, ear coverts and hindneck grey, throat plain buff (see juv. Grey Heron). **Status:** Locally common resident. More terrestrial than the similar-looking Grey Heron, nesting in loose mixed colonies. **Habitat:** Damp grasslands and cultivated areas near water. **Voice:** A croaking, frog-like call.

Goliath Heron
Ardea goliath

135–150cm Sexes similar. Largest heron in the world. Upperparts slate-grey; head, neck and underparts chestnut. Long legs are black, as is the large, deep bill; eyes are yellow. White foreneck and upper breast streaked black. Juv. duller, upperparts grey with rusty, scalloped feather edges; underparts streaked white. **Status:** Uncommon resident, usually solitary, often active nocturnally. **Habitat:** Large floodplains and major river valley systems. **Voice:** Hoarse croak, sometimes in flight.

Great Egret
Ardea alba

85–95cm Sexes similar. Largest white egret, with long slender neck held in characteristic S-shaped position. Long legs and feet are black, and bill is yellow with gape extending behind yellow eye. (Gape does not extend beyond eye in smaller Intermediate Egret.) Br. bird has black bill, lime-green facial skin and red eyes. Juv. similar to non-br. adult. **Status:** Common resident close to any water. Normally seen singly, unless breeding **Habitat:** Dams, large rivers and floodplains with shallow to deep water. **Voice:** Harsh croaking when breeding and in flight.

Intermediate Egret
Ardea intermedia

60–72cm Sexes similar. Slightly taller than Little Egret. All white with yellow eye and bill. Lower legs are black and upper legs diagnostic yellow to yellow-green. Gape does not extend behind eye (as in Great Egret). Br. bird has orange-red eye and bill, lime-green lores, reddish upper legs and develops plumes on back. Juv. similar to non-br. adult. **Status:** Widespread resident. Most common on Kafue Flats, Liuwa Plains and Bangweulu. **Habitat:** Marshy ground or shallowly inundated vegetation. **Voice:** An extended harsh croak.

Black Heron
Egretta ardesiaca

50–60cm Sexes similar. Small, slaty-black heron with long plumes on back of head; eyes dark. Legs black with bright yellow feet. Often forms umbrella with wings over head when feeding. Feet red during courtship. Juv. duller, browner without head plumes. **Status:** Occurs year-round. A wanderer. Breeding resident in Lochinvar and Bangweulu, often in mixed colonies. **Habitat:** Shallow waters in lagoons and floodplains. **Voice:** Croaking call around nest site.

Roddy Smith

Little Egret
Egretta garzetta

55–65cm Sexes similar. Small, slender white egret. Eyes yellow, dagger-like bill and legs black. Bright yellow feet diagnostic. Br. birds have long ornamental plumes on head, breast and back, and orange-red eyes and legs. Juv. with pale yellow-green lores and legs. **Status:** Common widespread resident but does wander. **Habitat:** Variety of wetlands with shallow water including rivers, lakes, floodplains and dams. **Voice:** Various harsh croaking sounds when breeding colonially.

Hamerkop
Scopus umbretta

50–58cm Sexes similar. Unmistakable dark brown bird. Head, with backward pointing crest and long, flat black bill, appears hammer-shaped. Juv. similar to adult. **Status:** A widely distributed resident. Usually solitary or in pairs. **Habitat:** Variety of aquatic habitats such as smaller rivers and streams, quiet backwaters, muddy edges of lagoons and pans, and seasonally flooded dambos where it builds its iconic, massive domed nest. **Voice:** Loud, raucous series of yipping notes, often given in flight.

Shoebill   *Balaeniceps rex*

120cm Sexes similar. Unmistakable, huge blue-grey bird. Small, erect crest on back of head. Massive yellow-grey bill with curved hook at the tip. **Status:** Vulnerable. Resident and mainly solitary. Breeding resident in Bangweulu with large territory requirement. Wanders to other swampy areas. **Habitat:** Papyrus swamps, inundated reeds and sedges. **Voice:** Mainly silent. Bill-clattering at nest.

Charles J. Sharp / CC BY-SA

Great White Pelican   *Pelecanus onocrotalus*

140–178cm Sexes similar. Large, all-white bird except for black primary and secondary feathers. Short crest at the back of head; bare facial skin pink. Bill and bill pouch yellow. When breeding, forehead swells and facial skin turns yellow in male and orange in female. In flight, pure white plumage contrasts with black flight feathers. Juv. has buffy-brown appearance. **Status:** Primarily a non-br. migrant from May to December with some remaining year-round. **Habitat:** Occurs on shallow waters on large floodplains. **Voice:** Mainly silent.

Reed Cormorant   *Microcarbo africanu*

50–60cm Sexes similar. Small cormorant with long tail and short bill. Br. birds are glossy black with red eye, orange facial skin and small crest on forehead. Non-br. birds duller with pale underparts, red-brown eye, and smaller crest. Juv. dull brown above with whitish underparts and no crest. **Status:** Common throughout; scarce in Luangwa Valley. Colonial breeder. **Habitat:** Lakes, dams, rivers, moves around waterbodies. **Voice:** Mainly silent; hisses and cackles at colonies.

White-breasted Cormorant
Phalacrocorax lucidus

80–100cm Sexes alike. Large cormorant with obvious white throat and breast. Head, hindneck and upperparts black; bronze tint on wings. White face has pink wash; eyes green. Br. bird shows white patch on the thighs. Non-br. birds browner and duller with no thigh patch. Imm. has entirely white underparts. **Status:** Locally common resident. **Habitat:** Large dams, rivers and floodplains. **Voice:** Normally silent. When breeding, gives a low guttural sound.

African Darter
Anhinga rufa

83–95cm This slender waterbird has a diagnostic long, thin neck with obvious kink, and a long pointed bill. Wings are black with white streaks. Br. male has rufous neck and white cheek stripe; mantle plumes become more obvious. Neck of female and non-br. male pale brown. Often sits with wings spread out to dry. Juv. similar to female, with whitish or pale buff underparts. **Status:** Widespread resident. **Habitat:** Larger rivers and floodplains, less common on dams. **Voice:** Mainly silent; makes croaking noises at the nest.

Secretarybird
Sagittarius serpentarius

125–150cm Sexes similar. A tall, unmistakable bird endemic to Africa with long legs, grey-and-black plumage and a diagnostic long, loose crest behind the head. Bare facial skin is orange, blue-grey bill short and hooked. In flight, long central tail feathers extend well beyond legs. Huge gape enables it to swallow large prey whole. Juv. with duller, brownish plumage and black bill. **Status:** Vulnerable. Distribution patchy; mainly on Kafue Flats and west of Zambezi. **Habitat:** Open grassland on edges of large dambos and floodplains. **Voice:** Usually silent. Makes croaking call displaying around nest.

Black-winged Kite   *Elanus caeruleus*

30–37cm Sexes similar. Small bird of prey, with broad white head and grey wings and back; black shoulder patch diagnostic. Large ruby-red eye. Underparts white, and white underwings tipped with black. Bill black, cere and legs yellow. Juv. has brown wash over body with white scalloped feathers and yellow-brown eyes. **Status:** Widespread resident. Greater numbers recorded mid-May to December. **Habitat:** Open country, tree savanna, grassland and cultivated areas. Perches on telephone poles. Hunts from perch or in hovering flight. **Voice:** Short, high whistle.

African Harrier-Hawk   *Polyboroides typus*

60–66cm Sexes similar. Large, grey, long-legged hawk. Small head with yellow facial skin, which flushes pinkish-red when agitated. Underparts finely barred black and white. Long, thin legs yellow. Underwing coverts barred black and white. Long tail black with distinctive broad, white central band and thin terminal band. Small head, bare face and shaggy nape are important identification characters. Juv. plumage variable, brown to mottled brown. **Status:** Locally common throughout. **Habitat:** Most woodland types including forest. **Voice:** Far-carrying plaintive whistle.

Hooded Vulture   *Necrosyrtes monachus*

65–75cm Sexes similar. Small, dark brown vulture with distinctive long, thin bill. Adult has white woolly down on back of head and nape. Facial skin flushes from pale to dark pink when agitated. White thighs most obvious in flight. Juv. dark brown (including thighs), with brown down on back of head and whitish facial skin. **Status:** Fairly common resident throughout. Most common in national parks. **Habitat:** Open woodland. **Voice:** Usually silent.

White-backed Vulture   *Gyps africanus*

90–95cm Sexes similar. Large vulture with brownish plumage, dark grey head and white down on neck. Eyes dark brown for all ages. White rump and lower back obvious in flight. Buffy-white underwing coverts contrast with blackish flight feathers. Juv. darker with white streaking on feathers and underwing coverts. **Status:** Widespread resident with some local wandering. **Habitat:** Open woodland. **Voice:** Hissing and harsh cackling when competing at carcasses.

White-headed Vulture
Trigonoceps occipitalis

78–85cm Sexes similar. Colourful vulture with white head, neck and legs. Bill orange-red, cere blue. Facial skin and neck pink. In flight, female shows white inner secondaries; male's grey-black secondaries extend into a thin white line across centre of wing. White belly obvious in both sexes. Juv. dark brown; face, neck and bill paler, with narrow white bar in middle of underwing extending to base of primaries. **Status:** Widespread but uncommon. **Habitat:** Woodland or savanna, but avoids dense woodland. **Voice:** Generally silent.

Michael Buckham

Lappet-faced Vulture   *Torgos tracheliotos*

98–115cm Sexes similar. Very large, all-dark vulture with white thighs. Diagnostic bare head and conspicuous neck folds (or lappets) red. Massive horn-coloured bill with blue-grey base. Underwings black with narrow white bar. White leggings and short, wedge-shaped tail aid identification. Juv. browner with paler facial skin; thighs brown. Adult plumage only reached around six years of age. **Status:** Fairly common resident. **Habitat:** Open woodland other than miombo. **Voice:** Generally silent.

Black-chested Snake Eagle
Circaetus pectoralis

60–68cm (wingspan 178cm) Sexes similar. Medium-sized eagle with black upperparts, white underparts and black breast. Eyes yellow; unfeathered legs grey. Underwings white with black barring on flight feathers. Juv. brown above, rufous-brown below, with faintly barred underwings and narrowly barred tail. **Status:** Widespread resident. **Habitat:** Open woodland and grassy plains, often hovers in high winds. **Voice:** Loud, high-pitched whistle in display flight.

Brown Snake Eagle   *Circaetus cinereus*

65–75cm (wingspan 164cm) Sexes similar. Largest snake eagle; uniformly dark brown. Large head, bright yellow eyes, dull white unfeathered legs; very upright posture diagnostic. Dark brown underwing coverts contrast with silvery-grey flight feathers; three to four narrow white bars on tail. Juv. variable, some similar to adult, others mottled on breast and abdomen. Similar-looking juv. Bateleur has dark brown eyes. **Status:** Widespread resident. **Habitat:** Most woodland types. Avoids heavily forested areas. **Voice:** Usually silent.

Western Banded Snake Eagle
Circaetus cinerascens

55–60cm (wingspan 114cm) Sexes similar. Stocky, medium-sized, grey-brown eagle. Light barring on lower breast, belly and flanks. Eyes pale yellow, cere and unfeathered legs yellow. Single broad white bar across centre of black tail diagnostic. Juv. brown, head streaked whitish, broad grey band on tail. **Status:** Locally fairly common. Scarce in the dry western parts and on plateau. **Habitat:** Riverine forest and woodland, along larger, well-wooded river systems. **Voice:** Loud, short series of whistles, often preceded by single note.

Ian Salisbury

Bateleur
Terathopius ecaudatus

55–70cm (wingspan 170–180cm)
Sexes similar. Adult unmistakable. Large and stocky with very short tail; facial skin and legs bright red. Head and underparts jet-black; back and tail chestnut. Rare morph has a cream back. Flight feathers all-black in male; female shows light grey wing panel. Male underwing white with broad black trailing edge; narrow black edge in female. Juv. all brown with greenish facial skin, legs white. **Status:** Near Threatened. Mainly in national parks and low-population areas. **Habitat:** Open woodland. **Voice:** A loud, harsh bark in aerial display.

Martial Eagle
Polemaetus bellicosus

78–86cm (wingspan 190–240cm)
Sexes similar. Huge eagle with dark brown head and upper breast, and lightly spotted white underparts. Head large with small crest and bright yellow eyes; legs are well feathered. In flight, underwings dark brown. Spotted, white underparts and feathered legs differentiate it from smaller Black-chested Snake Eagle. Juv. grey above, plain white below; eyes dark brown. **Status:** Vulnerable. Widespread resident. **Habitat:** Open woodland and plains. **Voice:** Loud whistles in aerial display.

Long-crested Eagle
Lophaetus occipitalis

53–58cm (wingspan 115cm)
Sexes similar. Dark brown eagle with distinctive large floppy crest. Male with white leggings, off-white to light brown in female. Broad, rounded wings with large white panels in primaries. Tail barred black and white. Eye, cere and feet yellow. Juv. similar but with grey eyes, shorter crest and upperparts speckled white and brown. **Status:** Widespread resident. Scarce in Luangwa Valley and Lower Zambezi. **Habitat:** Tall riparian woodland near marshy areas such as dambos. **Voice:** Long, plaintive whistle in aerial display.

imm.

Lesser Spotted Eagle   *Clanga pomarina*

55–67cm (wingspan 146–168cm)
Sexes similar. Dark brown with a diagnostic rounded crown with no crest, tightly feathered 'stovepipe trouser' legs, and a plain rounded tail. Eye yellow-brown. Similar Wahlberg's Eagle has small crest, brown eye and long, square tail. Juv. has white spots on upperwing coverts, and brown eye. In flight, shows narrow white line between flight feathers and wing coverts, and white crescent on rump. **Status:** Palaearctic migrant, from late October to March. Can be gregarious. **Habitat:** Well-wooded or open country. **Voice:** Silent when in Africa.

Wahlberg's Eagle   *Hieraaetus wahlbergi*

53–61cm (wingspan 130–146cm)
Sexes similar. Small eagle, with variable plumage from dark brown to pale buff. Easily confused with Lesser Spotted Eagle but small crest, baggy leg feathers (not 'stovepipe trousers') and dark brown eye are important distinguishing characteristics. Diagnostic straight-edged wings and narrow, square-ended tail in flight. Juv. resembles adult. **Status:** Common intra-African br. migrant, late July to April. **Habitat:** Any woodland especially miombo. **Voice:** Loud, mournful cry in flight, rapid yipping contact call at the nest.

Tawny Eagle   *Aquila rapax*

60–75cm (wingspan 170–200cm)
Sexes similar. Large eagle with variable plumage, from pale brown through reddish-brown to dark brown. No dark trailing edges to wings (see Steppe Eagle). Eye yellow-brown; yellow gape extends to centre of the eye (see Steppe Eagle). Tail long and rounded in flight. Juv. usually lighter in colour; eye dark brown. **Status:** Common in Luangwa Valley and the south, uncommon in other parts. Occurs singly or in pairs. **Habitat:** Open woodlands and woodland savanna. **Voice:** Short bark when breeding.

Steppe Eagle — *Aquila nipalensis*

72–81cm (wingspan 170–220cm) Sexes similar. Large all-brown eagle with ginger patch on nape. Eye brown. Diagnostic yellow fleshy gape extends to back of the eye (see Tawny Eagle). Black trailing edges to flight feathers and tail. Juv. cinnamon-brown with broad white band across upper- and underwing coverts, and prominent white crescent on rump. **Status:** Palaearctic migrant occurring from October to April. **Habitat:** Woodland habitats, particularly on central plateau. Gathers in large mixed groups at times of termite eruptions. **Voice:** Silent in Africa.

Nik Borrow

Verreaux's Eagle — *Aquila verreauxii*

80–90cm (wingspan 180–220cm) Sexes similar but female larger. Large, all-black eagle with distinctive white 'V' on back and white rump, visible mainly in flight. Eye dark brown, facial skin and feet yellow. Distinctive white panels in outer wing seen in flight. Juv. mottled brown and black with rufous crown and nape, and white primary 'windows'. **Status:** Resident, sparsely distributed. **Habitat:** Rocky escarpments and gorges, such as below Victoria Falls. **Voice:** A high-pitched whistle. Mainly silent.

African Hawk-Eagle — *Aquila spilogaster*

60–70cm (wingspan 142cm) Sexes similar. Medium-sized eagle with black head and upperparts, and clear white underparts moderately streaked. In flight and from above shows diagnostic white 'window' at base of primaries. Obvious black subterminal tail band. Juv. head and underparts rufous, upperparts brown, no subterminal band. **Status:** Widespread resident. **Habitat:** Open woodland and dry riverine forest **Voice:** A melodious whistle, usually given in display flight.

Lizard Buzzard   *Kaupifalco monogrammicus*

30–36cm Sexes similar. A small, squat raptor with grey upper body, head and breast. Diagnostic black stripe down white throat. Underparts white with fine grey barring. Rump white and tail with distinctive white bar (sometimes two). Cere pink to orange-red, eye and legs dark red. Juv. similar to adult with pale brown wash to underparts; brown eye; cere and legs paler. **Status:** Common resident. **Habitat:** Well-developed woodlands, particularly miombo. **Voice:** A loud, melodious whistle mainly in breeding season.

Gabar Goshawk   *Micronisus gabar*

28–36cm Sexes similar. A small raptor with grey upperparts, head and upper breast. White margin to secondaries and white rump conspicuous in flight. Underparts white with fine grey barring. Eye, cere and legs red. Uncommon black morph has black-and-white barring on underwing primaries, pale tail barring and no white rump. Juv. brown above, with streaked crown and breast, barred belly and black-ringed yellow eye. **Status:** Uncommon breeding resident. **Habitat:** Drier woodland habitats; scarce in Lower Zambezi. **Voice:** Piping notes mainly when breeding.

Inset: Grant Reed

Dark Chanting Goshawk
Melierax metabates

42–50cm Sexes similar. A small raptor with dark grey upperparts, head and breast; underparts finely barred, rump white with fine grey barring. Long legs and cere red; eye dark brown. Juv. brown above with white streaking on breast, brown barred belly and dark barring to pale rump; legs orange or dull yellow, eyes pale yellow, and cere grey or orange. **Status:** Common resident throughout. Uncommon in Luangwa Valley. **Habitat:** Broad-leaved woodland, particularly miombo. **Voice:** Calls mainly in the breeding season, a melodious whistle.

African Goshawk *Accipiter tachiro*

35–40cm Male dark-grey above, underparts white with fine rufous barring and rufous wash on underwing coverts. Two to three small white spots on top of central tail feathers. Female much larger, browner above with broader barring on underparts. Eye and legs yellow, cere greenish-grey. Juv. brown above with pear-shaped blotches on pale underparts, brown eye and white supercilium. **Status:** Widespread resident. **Habitat:** Well-wooded habitats. **Voice:** Clear, repetitive 'whik' given while circling in display flight, usually early mornings or when perched.

Shikra *Accipiter badius*

28–30cm Sexes similar. Small raptor with plain grey upperparts, grey central tail feathers (outer tail feathers barred) and plain grey rump. Underparts white with fine barring. Cere and legs yellow, eye coral-red (dark orange in female). Juv. grey-brown above with unstreaked crown, russet blotches on breast and barred belly; eyes yellow. Indistinct black line down centre of throat. **Status:** Common widespread resident. **Habitat:** Various woodland habitats including suburban gardens. **Voice:** Female gives drawn-out 'kiew'; male a sharp, repeated 'kewick'.

Little Sparrowhawk *Accipiter minullus*

20–25cm Sexes similar. Very small sparrowhawk, grey above and white below with fine brown barring. Female larger and slightly browner above. Combination of yellow eyes, cere and legs diagnostic. Rump white with two conspicuous white spots on uppertail. Juv. browner above; white underparts heavily marked with dark, pear-shaped brown spots. **Status:** Widespread throughout, apart from extreme southwest. **Habitat:** Densely wooded habitats, dry riparian forest. **Voice:** Noisy during breeding season. Series of high-pitched notes by male; female similar but softer.

Bernard Dupont

Casper Badenhorst

African Marsh Harrier · *Circus ranivorus*

44–49cm Sexes similar. Large harrier with dark brown body, rufous belly and thighs, and barred undertail and wing; white flecks on shoulder and white streaks on breast and flanks. Has owl-like facial ruff. Eyes and cere yellow, as are the long legs. Narrow long wings. Juv. dark brown with pale chest band; eyes brown; tail lightly barred. **Status:** Locally common in suitable habitat, apart from Luangwa Valley and Lower Zambezi. **Habitat:** Moist dambos, marshy areas with extensive *Phragmites* and *Typha* reedbeds. **Voice:** Seldom calls.

Yellow-billed Kite · *Milvus aegyptius*

50–60cm Sexes alike. All-brown raptor with yellow bill and cere. Tail forked. Juv. plumage variable with black-tipped bill, yellow cere and pale streaks on the head; dark eye mask and underparts. **Status:** Intra-African br. migrant occurring from July to March. **Habitat:** Open woodland; common near roadsides where it scavenges road kills. **Voice:** A soft, drawn-out trill.

juv.

African Fish Eagle · *Haliaeetus vocifer*

60–75cm (wingspan 175–210cm) Sexes similar. Distinctive eagle with diagnostic pure white head, breast and tail; bright yellow facial skin, black back, chestnut underparts. Dark eye at all stages. Female ten per cent larger than male and with more white on breast. Juv. mottled brown, black and white; white unbarred tail with dark terminal band. Takes four to five years to reach adult plumage. **Status:** Common resident. **Habitat:** Rivers lakes and dams. **Voice:** Loud, ringing call, often given in duet.

Common Buzzard (Steppe Buzzard)
Buteo buteo

45–52cm Sexes similar. Plumage variable; upperparts range from dark brown to rufous or grey-brown. White patch on breast. Pale rufous barring on belly. In flight, shows white panel in the wing. Upright posture when perched. Juv. underparts heavily streaked; white breast patch variable. **Status:** Palaearctic migrant from October to March. **Habitat:** Occurs mainly in open woodland habitats and on edges of exotic plantations. Regularly perches on trees, poles, posts, rocks and pylons. **Voice:** Silent while in Africa.

Casper Badenhorst

Augur Buzzard
Buteo augur

50–60cm (wingspan 130–145cm) Sexes similar. Large buzzard with black upperparts, white underparts and diagnostic brick-red tail. Broad white underwings have a black trailing edge and dark carpal patch. Female has black on lower throat. Juv. has brown upperparts with pale edged feathers and creamy-buff underparts, sometimes with rusty mottling. **Status:** Common in suitable mountainous areas. **Habitat:** Rocky hills and escarpments. **Voice:** A yelping courtship song.

Denham's Bustard
Neotis denhami

90–110cm A big bustard, male much larger than female. Pale head has black-and-white stripes. Male has an obvious orange patch on hindneck; less prominent in female. Female has fine buffy bars on foreneck. Both sexes have a large mottled black-and-white panel on wing, grey foreneck and white belly. Imm. similar to female. **Status:** Fairly widespread in suitable habitats. **Habitat:** Extensive open grasslands. **Voice:** Generally silent. Deep booming during display.

Black-bellied Bustard   *Lissotis melanogaster*

60–80cm A long-legged bustard with a long, thin neck. Male has white cheeks, and a dark crown and nape. Neck buff with black line from chin to breast; upperparts dark buff with clear black chevrons. Female buff with whitish belly; no dark head markings or black line on neck. Juv. similar to female but head and neck rust-coloured. **Status:** Locally common. **Habitat:** Open grassland, savanna woodland including miombo, and long grass on margins of dambos. **Voice:** Loud croak followed by popping sound.

African Finfoot   *Podica senegalensis*

52–65cm A large waterbird with distinctive bright orange-red bill and legs. Male with dark grey head and narrow white line running down neck; eye dark. Female with brown head and neck, white throat, and pale eye. Juv. resembles female but is browner and less spotted, white line on the neck absent, bill dark. **Status:** Resident. Secretive, often overlooked. **Habitat:** Permanent streams, rivers, pools with well-vegetated banks, particularly with reeds and overhanging tree branches. **Voice:** Mostly silent. Clicking or knocking sound.

African Crake   *Crex egregia*

20–23cm Sexes similar. A medium-sized crake with upperparts heavily streaked brown and black, noticeable in flight. Face, throat and breast grey. Distinctive black-and-white barring on belly and flanks. Eye red with red eye-ring, bill red with black tip. Juv. duller and darker. **Status:** Locally common intra-African br. migrant occurring from December to April. Uncommon in Lower Zambezi. Secretive habits. **Habitat:** Open, seasonally waterlogged grassland. **Voice:** Rapid rattling call, even in flight.

Black Crake
Amaurornis flavirostra

19–23cm Sexes similar. A small crake with all-black plumage, bright red eye and legs, and lemon-yellow bill. Juv. olive-brown above, dark grey below; bill initially horn-coloured, later turning black. **Status:** Very common resident with occasional local wandering. Unlike other crakes, frequently comes into the open. **Habitat:** Wetlands with tangled vegetation including reeds, sedges, papyrus and floating vegetation such as waterlilies. **Voice:** A diagnostic duet of strange growls, whistles and clucks.

African Swamphen
Porphyrio madagascariensis

38–50cm Sexes similar. A large gallinule with purple underparts, greenish back, massive red bill with red frontal shield, bright red legs and long toes. Juv. dark brown above, wings with greenish wash; bill and frontal shield blackish-red, legs and feet dull red. **Status:** Locally common resident. **Habitat:** Permanent waterbodies with extensive areas of tall vegetation such as *Typha* and Papyrus. **Voice:** A noisy bird. Loud croaks and grunts.

Lee Gutteridge

Allen's Gallinule
Porphyrio alleni

25–28cm Sexes similar. A small waterbird with dark blue head, neck and underparts, and olive-green upperparts; undertail coverts white. Br. bird has red eye, bill and legs; male frontal shield blue, female lime-green. Non-br. bird has brown shield and eye, and dull red legs. Juv. with upperparts mottled brown, underparts paler, bill red-brown, legs brown. **Status:** Locally common breeding visitor during rains, mid-December to April. Some overstay. **Habitat:** Temporary pools with rank grass, sedges and reedbeds interspersed with patches of open water with waterlilies and aquatic plants. **Voice:** Repetitive loud cluck.

Common Moorhen   *Gallinula chloropus*

30–36cm Sexes similar. A sooty-black waterbird with brown wash on wing and bold white streaks on folded wing and flank. Diagnostic red bill with yellow tip, has a large red frontal shield. Eyes are dark red and legs yellow-green; upper half of tibia is distinctive orange. Juv. dull brown, with greenish-brown frontal shield. **Status:** Common resident feeding on invertebrates and plants. **Habitat:** Freshwater wetlands with fringing emergent vegetation. **Voice:** Various grating and clucking notes.

Grey Crowned Crane   *Balearica regulorum*

100–110cm Sexes similar. A distinctive crane with diagnostic crown of stiff golden feathers. The black-and-white head has a red throat wattle. Neck and upperparts grey and wing coverts white. Underparts dark grey, tail black. Long black legs. Juv. with smaller crest, and lacks red wattle and black-and-white head markings. **Status:** Endangered. Locally common. Zambian population significant. Occurs in pairs or in flocks of some 50 up to 500. **Habitat:** Wetlands and open grassland, oxbow lagoons, roosts in trees. **Voice:** Loud, two-syllable trumpet.

Wattled Crane   *Grus carunculata*

130–175cm Sexes similar. Very large crane with long white neck, white upper breast, black belly and grey upperparts. Long white wattles on sides of face, bright red wart-like skin at base of the bill. Juv. is similar but paler, with no red facial skin and short wattles. **Status:** Significant resident population in Zambia, vulnerable elsewhere. Usually in pairs or fairly large flocks. **Habitat:** Large wetlands such as Kafue Flats and Bangweulu Swamp, and wet grasslands and dambos on central plateau. **Voice:** Bell-like honk.

Water Thick-knee *Burhinus vermiculatus*

38–41cm Sexes similar. A medium-sized wader with olive-brown upperparts with fine black streaking. Breast is buff with heavy streaks, belly white. Grey panel on wing with a thin white bar above, seen at rest and in flight. Juv. resembles adult but has brown flecks on the wing coverts. **Status:** Mainly resident with some local movements during high water levels. **Habitat:** Banks of lakes and large rivers with suitable vegetation to hide in during day. Always associated with water. **Voice:** Loud, piping whistle increasing in volume then falling off towards end. Calls mainly at night.

Spotted Thick-knee   *Burhinus capensis*

37–44cm Sexes similar. A medium-sized wader with clearly spotted buff upperparts. Face and breast heavily streaked. Large yellow eyes; bill black with yellow base. Juv. similar to adult but more streaked (less spotted) above. **Status:** Common resident in open woodlands in drier zones, congregating when non-br. **Habitat:** Stony, open areas in short grassland and woodland edges. Often on gravel roads at night. **Voice:** Mournful piping, rising then falling towards end. Calls mainly at night.

Black-winged Stilt   *Himantopus himantopus*

35–40cm Sexes similar. Distinctive long-legged wader. Male black above, white below with ruby-red eye and very long, thin black bill. Wings often show greenish gloss. Very long pink legs project well beyond the tail in flight. Non-br. bird has pale grey crown. Female alike but with duller brownish wings; upperparts duller with no greenish gloss. Juv. head and nape grey, upperparts brownish-black; white trailing edge to wings; legs grey with pink wash. **Status:** Widespread resident. **Habitat:** Lagoons, pans, lakes, floodplains, quiet stretches of rivers and dams. **Voice:** Sharp, repetitive yipping.

Long-toed Lapwing   *Vanellus crassirostris*

29–31cm Sexes similar. This lapwing has a striking white face, neck and throat, a black hindneck and breast, and a white belly. Upperparts grey-brown. Bill black with dark pink base; eye dark red with purple-pink eye-ring. Legs red with very long toes. Short carpal spurs. In flight, wings white except for black outer three primaries. Juv. similar to adult but browner upperparts mottled. **Status:** Resident with some local movement. **Habitat:** Swampy areas with extensive floating vegetation and muddy fringes. **Voice:** High-pitched, rapid chitter.

Blacksmith Lapwing   *Vanellus armatus*

28–31cm Sexes similar. Distinctive, medium-sized black, grey and white bird with a white crown, and a black face and neck. Bill and legs black. Male has long black carpal spurs. Juv. has greyish-brown upperparts with buffy tips, and a brownish crown. **Status:** Resident, some movement during rains. **Habitat:** Major river valley systems; short grassland; edges of floodplains, lakes and dams. **Voice:** Shrill 'tink' rising and falling in pitch and speed.

White-crowned Lapwing   *Vanellus albiceps*

28–32cm Sexes similar. A medium-sized lapwing with obvious, long yellow wattles. Crown white, head and neck grey, underparts all-white. Back brown, wings black and white, and outer three primaries black. Eye and legs yellow. Both sexes have long carpal spurs. Juv. with brownish-white crown; upperpart feathers with buffy fringes. **Status:** Common resident in Luangwa Valley and Lower Zambezi, in pairs or small groups. **Habitat:** Sandbanks of Luangwa and Zambezi rivers. **Voice:** Loud, high-pitched piping varying in pitch and speed.

Crowned Lapwing *Vanellus coronatus*

29–31cm Sexes similar. A medium-sized lapwing with distinctive black crown cap surrounded by white circle, ending in 'V' at the back of the head. Upperparts brown, belly white, bill and legs pinkish-red. Juv. with brown (not black) crown; upperparts with buffy fringes to feathers. **Status:** Common in dry parts of south and west, Bangweulu wetlands, and far north. Often in groups. **Habitat:** Short, dry grassland in floodplains, edges of dambos, and bare ground around cultivation and airstrips. **Voice:** Loud, repetitive screech, especially in flight.

African Wattled Lapwing
Vanellus senegallus

34–35cm Sexes similar. Largest lapwing in Zambia. Brown streaking on head extends down neck; white patch on forehead. Bright yellow wattles with red base diagnostic; bill yellow with black tip. Breast grey and upperparts brown. Legs bright yellow. Juv. similar with small wattles and streaked forehead, paler yellow legs. **Status:** Common resident, with post-br. congregations. **Habitat:** Wet grasslands and marshy areas. **Voice:** Noisy high-pitched cheeping, often at night.

Kittlitz's Plover *Charadrius pecuarius*

14–16cm Sexes similar. Small plover with mottled, dark brown upperparts, buffy underparts and white to buffy neck collar. Distinctive white or buffy-white supercilium extends to neck collar, and black eye-stripe extends down sides of the head. Juv. lacks eye-stripe and black collar. **Status:** Dry season breeding visitor (April to December) with some remaining during rains. **Habitat:** Open dry mud and short grass on the edge of lakes, dams and rivers. **Voice:** Either a fairly rapid chipping call or a double-note 'tu-lit'.

Three-banded Plover   *Charadrius tricollaris*

18cm Sexes similar. A small plover with diagnostic double black breast band. The face is grey with distinctive red eye-ring, black-and-red bill, and white forecrown; a white supercilium extends to back of the head. Belly white. Juv. duller with scalloped pale edges to upper body feathers; eye dark. **Status:** Common resident but with complex local movements while following water. **Habitat:** Shoreline of dams, rivers, streams and pans. Also artificial dams and sewage works. **Voice:** High-pitched chipping, also a double-note flight call.

Greater Painted-Snipe
Rostratula benghalensis

23–28cm Male with grey-brown head and golden upperwing coverts. Female with dark rufous head, neck and chest, uniform upperparts, and bronze-green wash with fine black bands on wing. Both sexes have white eye patch; black-and-white chest band extends up to mantle. Bill is fairly long and decurved. Juv. similar to adult male with paler spots on wing coverts. **Status:** Uncommon resident, movement linked to rainfall. **Habitat:** Marshes, flooded grasslands and edges of rivers. **Voice:** Double-note hoot by female.

Lesser Jacana   *Microparra capensis*

15–16cm Sexes similar. A very small wader with chestnut crown and hindneck. A narrow black or chestnut stripe through eye is diagnostic. Back of neck is blackish-brown. Wings have clear diagnostic white trailing edges in flight. Much smaller than even juv. African Jacana, with no frontal shield and shorter bill. Juv. duller with buff fringes to the upperpart feathers. **Status:** Scarce monogamous resident becoming nomadic if water levels drop. **Habitat:** Floodplains, pans and dambos with open pools and emergent vegetation, quiet backwaters of larger rivers. **Voice:** Soft repetitive hoot.

African Jacana
Actophilornis africanus

21–31cm Sexes similar. An unmistakable wader with long toes and striking diagnostic plumage: a chestnut body, black-and-white head, blue bill and obvious large blue frontal shield. Lacks trailing white edges to secondaries (see Lesser Jacana). Female larger than male. Juv. duller, with white eyebrow, thin black line through the eye, and light blue/grey frontal shield. **Status:** Widespread and common. Mainly resident but does move to seasonal pans. **Habitat:** Any waterbody with emergent vegetation, particularly waterlilies. **Voice:** A ringing or rasping call. Vocal when breeding.

Ruff
Calidris pugnax

Male 30cm, female 25cm Sexes similar. Non-br. adult with scaly or scalloped brown upperparts, grey head and breast with light streaks, and white underparts. Leg colour varies, from greenish-yellow to bright orange. Bill is short, dark and slightly decurved. Head small and neck long. Appearance is pot-bellied. A narrow white wingbar is visible in flight with white edges to rump and tail. Juv. buffy, otherwise similar to non-br. adult. **Status:** Common non-br. Palaearctic migrant. **Habitat:** Mudflats, wet grasslands, and dry floodplains. **Voice:** Mainly silent.

Little Stint
Calidris minuta

12–14cm Sexes similar. Tiny wader with variable plumage and short, straight black bill. Non-br. male has white forecrown and supercilium. Br. male has mottled greyish-brown upperparts, white underparts and fine streaking on sides of breast. In flight, shows narrow white wingbar, dark centre to rump and white edges to tail. Legs usually black, sometimes yellow-green. Juv. has buffy centre of crown, brown above and on breast; scapulars white with 'V' edges. **Status:** Common Palaearctic migrant in small flocks from August to April. Some remain year-round. **Habitat:** Wetland shorelines. **Voice:** High-pitched short 'chip'.

Michael Buckham

African Snipe *Gallinago nigripennis*

28–30cm Sexes similar. A wader with very long bill. Dark heavily marked upperparts contrast with white belly. Wing coverts are dark brown with pale buff edges. White trailing edge to wings in flight. Juv. similar to adult. **Status:** Widespread resident. Scarce in the east. **Habitat:** Dambos and marshes. **Voice:** Single 'tchuk' note when flushed. Drumming sound caused by wind passing through the fanned tail during aerial displays by males; monotonous 'chuck' given by females on the ground.

Common Sandpiper *Actitis hypoleucos*

19–21cm Sexes similar. A small shorebird with short legs, olive-brown upperparts, white underparts with diagnostic white crescent in front of folded wing. Bill black, legs greenish-grey. Bobs head and body and wags tail. Distinctive flight is rapid with shallow wing beat and glide. Shows white wingbar and dark rump. Juv. similar but upperpart feathers have buff margins. **Status:** Widespread non-br. Palaearctic migrant with year-round records. **Habitat:** Sand or rocks along shores of dams, streams, and rivers. **Voice:** A high-pitched 'tsee-tsee-tsee'.

Lee Gutteridge

Marsh Sandpiper *Tringa stagnatilis*

22–26cm Sexes similar. A medium shorebird with straight, thin black bill. Upperparts pale grey, forehead and underparts bright white. Black carpal patch on the folded wing. Legs greenish-yellow. In flight shows white back and rump; outer wing panels darker than inner. Juv. like adult but darker above. Common Greenshank much larger with slightly upturned, heavier bill. **Status:** Common non-br. Palaearctic migrant. **Habitat:** Saline wetlands, temporary pools in river floodplains, muddy fringes of open waterbodies. **Voice:** High-pitched single note on take-off.

Wood Sandpiper
Tringa glareola

19–22cm Sexes similar. Small shorebird with boldly spotted upperparts. Distinct white eyebrow extends behind eye. Short black bill. Long yellow-green legs project beyond tail in flight. In flight, shows pale underwings, white rump and fine barring on tail. Juv. browner above. **Status:** Common widespread non-br. Palaearctic migrant, mostly September to April. Many present year-round, either solitary or small groups. **Habitat:** Wide range of shoreline and freshwater habitats. **Voice:** A series of high-pitched chittering notes, usually given on take-off.

Common Greenshank
Tringa nebularia

30–35cm Sexes similar. Waterbird with long, slightly upturned bill, dark lores and indistinct supercilium. Upperparts grey, white below. Long grey-green legs. In flight shows extensive white back and rump, no wingbar. Juv. similar with browner upperparts, neck and breast more streaked. **Status:** Common Palaearctic migrant with wide distribution. Many birds remain year-round. **Habitat:** Muddy or sandy edges of waterbodies including dams, ponds and rivers. **Voice:** Fairly rapid, distinctive three- to four-note whistle, 'tieuw-ieuw-tieuw', usually given in flight.

Lee Gutteridge

Temminck's Courser
Cursorius temminckii

19–21cm Sexes similar. Small courser with rufous crown, broad black stripe running from behind eye to nape, and clear white eye-stripe above it. Upperparts and breast are light brown; black patch on belly. Legs white. Juv. has black-and-brown mottling on the upperparts, belly brown. **Status:** Breeding visitor in dry season occurring mainly July to December. Some present during rains. Occurs in pairs and family groups. Diurnal. **Habitat:** Freshly burned ground; also short, open grassland, dry margins of dambos, fallow cultivation and airfields. **Voice:** Grating 'err-err' given in flight.

Three-banded Courser *Rhinoptilus cinctus*

25–28cm Sexes similar. This courser has a mottled crown, broad white supercilium, chestnut bands on neck and lower breast, and black band mid-chest. Bill is yellow with a black tip. Legs pale yellow. Juv. similar to adult, but chestnut bands faint or absent. **Status:** Resident in south and east including Lower Zambezi and Luangwa Valley. Occurs in pairs or family groups. Predominantly nocturnal. **Habitat:** Woodland, particularly mopane woodland. **Voice:** Mainly silent. Loud, high pitched piping notes when breeding.

Bronze-winged Courser
Rhinoptilus chalcopterus

26–28cm Sexes similar. Largest courser. Distinctive brown-and-white face markings. Eye-ring and long legs red. Clear black breast band. Metallic-bronze or violet tips to primary feathers. Juv. duller with narrower breast band, less distinctive face markings. **Status:** Both resident and intra-African br. migrant. Influx between April and December. Usually in pairs. Nocturnal. **Habitat:** Open woodland, particularly mopane, bare patches and recently burnt ground. **Voice:** Plaintive, piping three-note call, usually given at night

Roddy Smith

Collared Pratincole *Glareola pratincol*

22–25cm Sexes similar. This pratincole has long slender wings, a deeply forked tail, and rapid, agile flight. The buffy-yellow throat has a narrow black border; breast brown, belly white. In flight shows reddish-brown underwing coverts and white tips to the secondary feathers. Bill red with black tip. Juv. similar but lacks black throat border. **Status:** Occurs year-round with some local movement. Highly gregarious. **Habitat:** Edges of floodplains, lakes, large rivers and dams. **Voice:** Various shrill or trilled notes.

Rock Pratincole
Glareola nuchalis

18–20cm Sexes similar. Small pratincole with grey-brown upperparts, dark brown cap, white neck collar, red bill with a black tip, and short, red legs. Tail short with narrow fork. In flight shows narrow white underwing bar. Rump and uppertail coverts white. Juv. lacks white collar and has duller legs and buffy scalloped edges to body feathers. **Status:** Intra-African br. migrant occurring late July to March, departing when rivers flood. **Habitat:** Restricted to exposed isolated rocks in large rivers where it breeds. **Voice:** A high-pitched chipping call.

African Skimmer
Rynchops flavirostris

36–42cm Sexes similar. A striking bird with black-and-white plumage, huge bright red bill with yellow tip, and red legs. Wings long and slender with white trailing edge. Juv. mottled brown and grey above, bill paler. **Status:** Congregates along major sandy rivers in fairly large numbers. Breeding success fluctuates due to boating and fish-netting disruptions. Non-breeders are nomadic along most waterbodies. Mostly crepuscular or nocturnal. **Habitat:** Major rivers with sandbanks devoid of vegetation. **Voice:** Sharp trill in flight.

Casper Badenhorst

Casper Badenhorst

Grey-headed Gull
Chroicocephalus cirrocephalus

40–42cm Sexes similar. This gull has an all-grey head when breeding, limited grey when non-br. Neck, tail and underparts are white, wings and back grey, bill and legs red, and eye pale yellow. Juv. has brown markings on the head, mantle and wing coverts. Bill is pinkish. **Status:** Common resident. Large numbers congregate around hydroelectricity turbine outlets to feed on fish remains. Dry season influx, mainly April to November. Monogamous colonial breeder. **Habitat:** Lakes and large rivers. Scarce in Luangwa Valley. **Voice:** Loud croaks.

non-br.

br.

Nik Borrow

Whiskered Tern
Chlidonias hybrida

25–26cm Sexes similar. A small freshwater tern with diagnostic br. plumage – black crown and nape, white cheek, dark grey underparts and crimson bill and legs. Non-br. with white vent, grey rump (white in White-winged Tern); white underparts; fine streaking on crown, black patch behind eye, and black bill and legs. Juv. with brown tips to mantle and scapular feathers. Easily confused with White-winged Tern in non-br. plumage. **Status:** Common resident, monogamous and opportunistic small colonial breeder. **Habitat:** Freshwater lakes, pans and rivers. **Voice:** Harsh rasping.

br.

non-br.

Alexey Sokolov 1971 / CC BY-SA

Imran Shah / CC BY-SA

White-winged Tern
Chlidonias leucopterus

20–23cm Sexes similar. Small freshwater tern with distinctive br. plumage: black head and body, white rump, grey upperwing with white coverts. Bill and legs reddish-black. Non-br. is pale grey above, white below, with white rump and tail. (Grey rump in Whiskered Tern.) Obvious black ear patch extends below eye. Juv. with brown saddle on back and silver-grey wings. **Status:** Abundant non-br. Palaearctic migrant occurring mainly November to May. **Habitat:** Lakes and swamps such as Bangweulu and Kafue Flats. **Voice:** Series of hoarse notes.

♀

♂

Lee Gutteridge x2

Yellow-throated Sandgrouse
Pterocles gutturalis

28–30cm Largest African sandgrouse with dark chestnut underwings and belly conspicuous in flight. Face and throat yellow, lores black. Male with diagnostic broad black collar on throat. Female with streaked breast and mottled black-and-brown back. Juv. has smaller spots and narrower bars on upperparts. **Status:** Intra-African br. migrant in dry season from April to December, in pairs and small groups. Status threatened by constant fires in floodplains. **Habitat:** Extensive dry floodplains in south and west. **Voice:** Deep two-note frog-like croak 'aug-aug'.

Double-banded Sandgrouse
Pterocles bicinctus

25–26cm The male is distinguished by a black-and-white band on forehead and across chest. Neck and throat are buffy yellow, underparts barred. Female has barred upper breast. Upperparts also barred, with black, pale chestnut and buff mottling. Juv. similar to female with less barring and buff edges to feathers. **Status:** Fairly common resident. Occurs in pairs or small groups drinking at dusk. **Habitat:** Mopane woodlands in southern Zambia and Luangwa Valley. **Voice:** Mellow whistles called by a flock.

Mourning Collared Dove
Streptopelia decipiens

28–30cm Sexes similar. A pale grey dove. Yellow eye and red eye-ring diagnostic. Black collar with white margin on neck. Shows white in outer tail feathers in flight. Juv. browner, eye pale brown. **Status:** Common resident in Luangwa Valley, Lower Zambezi and parts of the south and west. **Habitat:** Riverine *Acacia* woodlands especially Winterthorn (*Faidherbia albida*) concentrations. **Voice:** Three- to four-note cooing; loud, growling call, particularly when landing.

Red-eyed Dove   *Streptopelia semitorquata*

32–35cm Sexes similar. Largest dove with black collar, pinkish wash to the breast and underparts, and dark red eye with purple-red eye-ring. In flight shows neither white outer tail feathers (see Ring-necked Dove) nor white tips to tail. Juv. lacks black collar, has grey skin around eye and mottled upperparts. **Status:** Widespread resident. **Habitat:** Riverine woodland and forest; also common in exotic plantations and suburban gardens. **Voice:** Loud series of far-carrying, deep coos. Harsh, growling call during courtship.

Ring-necked Dove   *Streptopelia capicola*

25–27cm Sexes similar. A blue-grey dove with distinct black neck collar and a pale pink wash on neck and breast. White outer tail feathers obvious in flight (see Red-eyed Dove). Eye dark brown or black with no red eye-ring. Juv. lacks black collar. Underpart feathers have buffy edges. **Status:** Very common widespread resident. **Habitat:** Open woodland, cultivated areas and gardens in villages and towns. Avoids forest and dense woodland. **Voice:** Loud three- to four-note crowing 'kuk-koorr-ko', often repeated many times. Harsh growling call when alighting.

Laughing Dove   *Spilopelia senegalensis*

22–24cm Sexes similar. A familiar dove with distinctive pale pink head and neck, and dark pink or rufous breast with black speckled necklace. No black collar on hindneck. Wing coverts blue-grey, back brownish. In flight shows white outer tail feathers. Juv. breast is grey with no speckling; browner overall. **Status:** Common resident, sometimes in large congregations. **Habitat:** Drier woodlands especially *Acacia*, cultivated areas in villages and towns. Less common in miombo woodlands. **Voice:** Soft six- to eight-note cooing, sounds like laughing.

Emerald-spotted Wood Dove
Turtur chalcospilos

18–20cm Sexes similar. A small dove with blue-grey head, light brown upperparts and two black bands on lower back. Iridescent emerald-green spots on the wings appear black in poor light. Bill is black. In flight shows rufous underwings. Juv. upper and underparts barred rufous; wing spots dull. **Status:** Common widespread resident; usually in pairs. **Habitat:** Most woodland types and gardens. **Voice:** Distinctive and melodious, soft long cooing, starting slowly and speeding up, then falling in pitch towards end.

Namaqua Dove
Oena capensis

26–28cm A small-bodied dove with a long, pointed tail. Upperparts grey-brown with three to five iridescent purple spots on wings. Underparts white. Primary feathers rufous in flight. Male has black face and throat, and orange bill with dark base. Female has no black on face and throat, and a brown bill. Juv. is barred black, with white and tan on upperparts and breast. **Status:** Common mainly March to November; sometimes solitary, often in pairs or flocks. **Habitat:** Open wooded grasslands and cultivated areas. **Voice:** Soft, mournful extended coo.

African Green Pigeon
Treron calvus

25–28cm Sexes similar. A parrot-like pigeon with olive-green plumage, grey mantle, lilac shoulder patches and bright yellow leg feathers. Large bill is grey with red base; eye bluish-white. Juv. duller with no lilac shoulder patches. **Status:** A common resident that wanders widely in search of fruiting trees. Occurs seasonally in montane forest December to March. **Habitat:** Canopy of dense woodland including miombo and *Combretum*, riverine forest especially where there are figs (*Ficus* species) **Voice:** Combination of deep growls and fluty trills.

Schalow's Turaco
Tauraco schalowi

41–44cm Sexes similar. This colourful fruit-eating bird has a long, pointed green crest with white tips, dark blue to violet tail, and green head, mantle and breast. It has a red eye-ring, white line under the eye and a dull red bill. Bright red primary feathers are obvious in flight. Juv. is duller with brownish bill and bare skin around the eyes. **Status:** Widespread localised resident. **Habitat:** Upper levels of evergreen forest, riparian feeding along rivers, and miombo woodland. **Voice:** Slow sequence of harsh growling notes.

Stephanie McDougall

Purple-crested Turaco
Tauraco porphyreolophus

42–46cm Sexes similar. A turaco with rounded purple crest, metallic-green face, olive-green mantle and olive breast with rose-pink wash. Back and wing coverts are greyish-blue. Bright red primary feathers very obvious in flight. Rump and tail dark blue-black, bill black. Juv. similar but duller with less red on underwings.
Status: Localised common resident.
Habitat: Thickets, dense woodland including riparian and miombo, sometimes gardens.
Voice: Repeated loud crowing notes rising in pitch and volume, ending abruptly.

Ross's Turaco
Musophaga rossae

50–54cm Sexes similar. This unmistakable turaco has purple plumage with a yellow bill, face patch and frontal shield, and a distinctive crimson crest. In flight shows crimson flight feathers. Juv. duller, with black forehead and facial patch, and black crest with red central patch. **Status:** Locally common resident in northern half of country. Confirmed sightings on lower Kafue River. **Habitat:** Moist riparian and evergreen forest, large thickets in rich miombo. *Cryptosepalum* and *Marquesia* forest in northwest. **Voice:** Growling call, also duet – a cacophony of croaking notes.

Grey Go-away-bird
Corythaixoides concolor

47–50cm An unmistakable large all-grey bird with a long tail, and large, rather loose crest that is raised when bird is alarmed. Bill and legs are black. Juv. is paler with shorter crest and buffy tinge to plumage. **Status:** Common resident. Often in family groups. **Habitat:** Dry woodland savannas including *Acacia*, mopane and light miombo woodland. **Voice:** Distinctive high-pitched single note often changed to harsher 'kwe' or expanded 'kwe-awy' with or without harsh growling notes.

Senegal Coucal   *Centropus senegalensis*

38–40cm Sexes similar. This coucal has a plain, unbarred black rump distinguishing it from White-browed and larger Coppery-tailed coucals. Head and nape are black, back and wings rufous, tail black, and underparts creamy white. Eye is red, bill black. Juv. has a horn-coloured bill, grey or brown crown, black and brown barring on upperparts, and buffy underparts. Eye is grey, changing to light brown. **Status:** Widespread resident. **Habitat:** Long grass and thickets in woodland, edges of reedbeds. **Voice:** Steady bubbling call, sometimes in duet.

Coppery-tailed Coucal
Centropus cupreicaudus

48–52cm Sexes similar. Largest coucal with heavy black bill. Head and tail black with coppery sheen more noticeable in good light. Back is dark rufous. Uppertail coverts are finely barred (Senegal Coucal shows no barring). Underparts are creamy white. Juv. duller with no coppery sheen. **Status:** Locally common in north and west. Absent from Lower Zambezi and Luangwa Valley. **Habitat:** Tall reedbeds and papyrus (*Cyperus papyrus*). **Voice:** Deep, rather slow bubbling call.

Dori McDougall

White-browed Coucal
Centropus superciliosus

36–42cm Sexes similar. A large coucal with distinct white eyebrow, creamy-white streaks on head and neck, and finely barred rump. Upperparts are rich chestnut. (Similar-looking Senegal Coucal has no white eyebrow and unbarred rump.) Juv. has streaked upperparts, barred back and buff eyebrow. **Status:** Locally common in eastern half of Zambia and larger rivers in west. **Habitat:** Moist lowland vegetation, tall rank grass, marshes and thickets; also montane areas in bracken–briar. **Voice:** Loud, rapid bubbling call.

Roy Glasspool

Black Coucal
Centropus grillii

35–38cm Sexes similar. The br. adult is black with chestnut wings. Non-br. plumage is dark brown above with rufous barring and buff below. Uppertail coverts are black with narrow buff bars. Juv. is streaked above, with barred wings, tail and rump. **Status:** Intra-African br. migrant, tends to be nomadic. A polyandrous species, male performs all nest duties. **Habitat:** Seasonally inundated floodplains and dambos favouring tall rank grass. **Voice:** Double-note popping. Also gulping call with uncertain purpose.

Casper Badenhorst

juv.

Great Spotted Cuckoo
Clamator glandarius

38–42cm Sexes similar. A large cuckoo with long wings, silvery-grey crest, buff throat, white underparts and dark brown upperparts with white spots. Juv. crest and face are black, flight feathers rufous and underparts buffy. **Status:** Common intra-African br. migrant. Present September to May. Parasitises mainly Pied Crow and Meves's Starling. **Habitat:** Semi-arid open woodland, particularly well-developed *Acacia*. **Voice:** Chattering call varying in tempo and pitch.

Levaillant's Cuckoo
Clamator levaillantii

38–40cm Sexes similar. A large cuckoo with distinctive black crest and upperparts, heavily streaked white throat and breast, and long white-tipped tail. (Similar-looking Jacobin Cuckoo shows no streaking on underparts.) Juv. has dark brown upperparts, buffy underparts, indistinct streaking on breast, and black bill (bill yellow in juv. Jacobin Cuckoo). **Status:** Widespread intra-African br. migrant occurring October to early May. Parasitises Arrow-marked and Hartlaub's babblers. **Habitat:** Woodland and riverine habitats. **Voice:** A loud whistle followed by a rapid series of harsh notes.

Jacobin Cuckoo
Clamator jacobinus

34cm Sexes similar. A black-and-white cuckoo with distinct black crest and white patches on wings. Breast all-white (striped in Levaillant's Cuckoo). Uncommon all-black morph. Juv. black above with buffy tip to tail, bill light yellow/brown. **Status:** Widespread intra-African br. migrant from September to mid-May. **Habitat:** Wide range of woodland habitats. Mainly parasitises both species of bulbul, and Sombre Greenbul. **Voice:** Loud, ringing three- to four-note call, often followed by a series of guttural notes.

Lee Gutteridge

Diederik Cuckoo
Chrysococcyx caprius

17–20cm Male metallic-green above with white stripe behind and in front of the eye (see Klaas's Cuckoo). White spots on wings, broad green bars on flanks. Red eye and eye-ring. Female back bronzy, white spots on wings, dull green barring on flanks. Juv. dull green or coppery above with coral-red bill, dark streaks on white underparts. **Status:** Common intra-African br. migrant. Parasitises numerous hosts including weavers, bishops and buntings. **Habitat:** Woodland, grassland and gardens. **Voice:** A loud, persistent 'dee-dee-deederik'.

Lee Gutteridge x2

Klaas's Cuckoo
Chrysococcyx klaas

18cm Male has glossy green upperparts, white underparts and plain green wing. White spot only behind eye (see Diederik Cuckoo). Female is duller with bronzy wash to upperparts, and well-barred brownish head, breast and flanks; lacks white spots on wings. White outer tail feathers are visible in flight. Juv. is similar to female with barred underparts. **Status:** Common resident. Parasitises wide range of hosts including warblers, sunbirds, batises and crombecs. **Habitat:** Most woodland types apart from very dry habitats. **Voice:** A loud, repeated 'may-ee-kee may-ee-kee'.

Eric Alsworth-Elvey. Inset: Albert Froneman

African Emerald Cuckoo
Chrysococcyx cupreus

20–23cm Cuckoo with no white on wing or white spot behind eye (see Klaas's Cuckoo). Male has emerald-green head, breast and upperparts and bright yellow belly. Female has fine green-and-rufous barring on head, breast, upperparts and undertail. Juv. crown and nape barred white. **Status:** Locally common intra-African br. migrant. **Habitat:** Canopy of evergreen and deciduous forest, rich miombo or similar rich woodland, and well-wooded gardens. **Voice:** Loud, musical four-note whistle likened to 'pretty georgie'.

Black Cuckoo
Cuculus clamosus

28–30cm Sexes similar. All-black cuckoo with narrow white tip to tail and some faint white barring on undertail. Female may show some barring on the underparts. Juv. similar to adult but no white tip to tail. **Status:** Common intra-African br. migrant September to May. Parasitises wide range of species including Tropical Boubou, Crimson-breasted Shrike and African Golden Oriole. **Habitat:** Miombo and other open woodland types. **Voice:** A mournful two-note whistle, also rapid excited rising series of notes.

Red-chested Cuckoo
Cuculus solitarius

28–31cm Sexes similar though russet chest of female may be paler. Upperparts dark grey; dark brown bars on white or buff lower breast and belly. Juv. upperparts darker than adult, head and throat black. Underparts barred black and white. **Status:** Very common intra-African br. migrant occurring August to April. Main hosts are robins, thrushes and Boulder Chat. **Habitat:** Well-wooded areas including miombo, riverine vegetation, forest and gardens. **Voice:** A distinctive, loud, three-note whistle, repeated continuously. Often calls at night.

African Cuckoo *Cuculus gularis*

32cm Sexes similar. An ashy-grey cuckoo with clear broad white bars across undertail (small spots or thin bars in Common Cuckoo). Uppertail plain dark grey with dark terminal band (no terminal band in Common Cuckoo). Bill yellow with black tip. Female may show buff wash on breast. Juv. body heavily barred with brownish grey. **Status:** Common intra-African br. migrant between August and May. Parasitises Fork-tailed Drongo exclusively. **Habitat:** Dry and open woodland including miombo and mopane. **Voice:** Best identified by double-note 'hoop-hoop' call.

Common Cuckoo *Cuculus canorus*

32–34cm Sexes similar. A dark ashy-grey cuckoo, difficult to distinguish from very similar African Cuckoo. Underside of tail has small isolated spots and incomplete thin white bars; uppertail plain grey (see African Cuckoo). Bill black with yellow base. A red-brown morph of female occurs. Juv. underparts predominantly grey, with barred rufous head and neck (whiter face in Common Cuckoo), and rufous or brown marks on wing coverts and flight feathers. **Status:** Palaearctic migrant from October to March. **Habitat:** Various open woodland types. **Voice:** Generally silent in Africa.

Western Barn Owl *Tyto alba*

35cm Sexes similar. A medium-sized pale owl with distinctive heart-shaped white facial disc. Upperparts are mottled buffy-orange and grey, underparts are whitish with small black spots on breast and flanks. Upper half of rim disc is buff, lower half dark brown. Eyes are black. Juv. similar to adult, darker grey above. **Status:** Common widespread resident. **Habitat:** Most woodland types; old buildings, roofs of houses, disused mine shafts and old Hamerkop nests. **Voice:** Eerie, loud, single screech, usually given in flight. Loud hissing young in nest.

Frank Rijnders

African Scops Owl · *Otus senegalensis*

15–17cm Sexes similar. A tiny, slender owl with distinctive ear tufts. Grey to grey-brown overall with fine black streaking and mottling. The pale grey facial disc has a narrow black rim. Eyes are yellow, bill blackish. (Southern White-faced Owl is much larger, with white face and orange eyes.) Juv. similar to adult with brown wash.
Status: Common widespread resident.
Habitat: Various woodlands, particularly miombo and *Acacia*, also gardens.
Voice: Loud, repetitive frog-like, single-note 'prrup'; a typical night sound.

Southern White-faced Owl · *Ptilopsis grant*

25–28cm Sexes similar. A medium-sized owl with pale grey upperparts streaked with black, and a white line across the shoulder. Grey underparts are finely barred with black streaks. The white facial disc has a clear black rim. Large, blackish ear tufts and orange eyes (African Scops Owl has grey face disc and yellow eyes). Juv. is browner with paler streaking and orange-yellow eyes.
Status: Uncommon unobtrusive resident.
Habitat: Wide range of woodland types, particularly *Acacia-Combretum*.
Voice: Series of soft bubbling notes.

Spotted Eagle-Owl · *Bubo africanus*

45cm Sexes similar. Large owl. Grey-brown upperparts with white spots and obvious ear tufts. Facial disc is grey outlined in black. Underparts are finely barred grey and white with brown blotches on breast. Eyes yellow and bill black. Juv. similar, ear tufts shorter. **Status:** Widely distributed resident. Often hunts along roads at night.
Habitat: Many woodland types, montane grassland, edges of farmland and gardens.
Voice: Two- to three-syllable hoot, second note lower; sometimes in duet.

Verreaux's Eagle-Owl
Bubo lacteus

58–66cm Sexes similar but female much larger. Largest African owl with short ear tufts and off-white facial disc with broad, black rim. Dark brown eyes have diagnostic pink eyelids. Bill is pale and horn-coloured. Upperparts are grey-brown; whitish underparts are finely barred milky grey. Juv. is pale grey-brown with broad bars; facial disc is less pronounced and ear tufts smaller. **Status:** Widespread but localised resident. **Habitat:** Favours tall riverine trees, especially *Acacia* species. **Voice:** Very deep grunts. Juv. plaintive repeated whistle after fledging, even in daylight.

Pel's Fishing Owl
Scotopelia peli

60–64cm Sexes similar. Very large owl with rufous upperparts showing narrow brown barring, and streaked and spotted paler underparts. Huge dark brown eyes and no ear tufts. Grey-brown legs are unfeathered. Juv. body and head have conspicuous whitish down with rufous wash. **Status:** Resident on all major rivers. Replaced by Vermiculated Fishing Owl in extreme northwest. **Habitat:** Permanent pools and dense fringing vegetation. **Voice:** Deep hoot, may be given in duet. Eerie loud wail is given by female soliciting food from male or by well-grown chick.

Sarah Solomon

African Wood Owl
Strix woodfordii

34cm Sexes similar. A medium-sized owl with large, dark brown eyes with narrow red eye rims. Facial disc is white. No ear tufts. Upperparts are rufous brown; white spots on wings and scapulars. Rufous underparts are heavily barred white. Bill and cere are deep yellow. Juv. similar to adult with pale rufous down. **Status:** Locally common resident. **Habitat:** Forests and densely wooded habitats. **Voice:** Series of rapid hoots by both sexes, with louder first hoot. Higher-pitched notes by female. Also gives a single hoot.

Pearl-spotted Owlet *Glaucidium perlatum*

18–19cm Sexes similar. A tiny owl. Upperparts including crown are brown with white spots. There are two brown 'false eyes' at the back of head; no ear tufts. Underparts are white with brown streaks. (African Barred Owlet is barred above, blotched below.) Eyes and bill yellow. Juv. similar but no spots on head and back. **Status:** Locally common resident in south and west, Luangwa Valley and extreme north. **Habitat:** Open woodland or wooded grassland. **Voice:** Long series of loud whistles given day and night.

African Barred Owlet *Glaucidium capense*

20–22cm Sexes similar. A small owlet. Large, rounded head has fine white barring and no ear tufts. Upperparts are finely barred brown with a conspicuous white scapular bar. Underparts are white with large brown blotches. Eyes are yellow, bill and cere grey-green. Juv. is less barred above, spotted below. **Status:** Resident. Common in suitable habitats. **Habitat:** Well-developed miombo, riverine woodland, edges of forest, and thickets. **Voice:** Loud, repetitive, ascending 'kroo, kroo, kroo' dropping off with 'prr-prr-prr'.

Rufous-cheeked Nightjar
Caprimulgus rufigena

23–24cm Sexes similar. Greyish upperparts with narrow black streaks. A thin orange-buff collar sits below a white throat patch. Narrow white line on scapulars. Rictal bristles are all dark (see Fiery-necked Nightjar). Male shows three white spots on folded wing, and small white tips to outer tail feathers, buff in female. Juv. similar to female. **Status:** Intra-African br. migrant August to April. Best identified by call. **Habitat:** Dry woodlands in west and south. **Voice:** Diagnostic continuous churring with no change in pitch (see Square-tailed Nightjar) preceded by a 'whoop'.

Lee Gutteridge

Fiery-necked Nightjar
Caprimulgus pectoralis

23–25cm Sexes similar. Stocky nightjar with large head, broad rufous neck collar and black-spotted scapulars; has diagnostic white bases to rictal bristles. Male has white wing spots on main flight feathers, female has buffy. White tail spots cover half of outer tail in male, but just the lower third in female. Juv. wing and tail spots buff. **Status:** Common widespread resident; often perches on low branches. **Habitat:** Any woodland, preferring miombo. **Voice:** Loud and clear two-note whistle or a similar melodious whistle ending in a trill.

Freckled Nightjar   *Caprimulgus tristigma*

26–28cm Sexes similar. Large nightjar with dark, cryptic 'freckled' or speckled coloration matching bare rocky habitat. No rufous collar, no wingbar. In flight, both sexes show white spots on primary feathers. Male has broad white tips to the outer tail feathers, absent in female. White spots on primaries absent in juv. **Status:** Widespread resident apart from rock-free Kalahari sand areas in west. Roosts by day on exposed rock or amongst rocky vegetation. **Habitat:** Bare rocky hills and escarpments in woodland areas. **Voice:** Repetitive, distinctive 'bow-wow'.

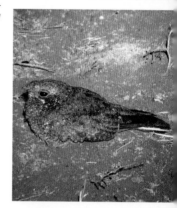

Square-tailed Nightjar   *Caprimulgus fossii*

23–24cm Sexes similar. Small, brownish-grey nightjar with narrow rufous neck collar and broad white (male) or buff (female) horizontal bar on shoulder. Tips of secondary feathers are white or buff creating a third wingbar. Diagnostic whole outer tail panel white (male) or buff (female). White or buff wing spots very distinctive in flight. Juv. similar to female. **Status:** Common widespread resident. **Habitat:** Open woodland and sandy country. Sparse in parts of northeast. **Voice:** Diagnostic loud, continuous churring song rising and falling in pitch (see Rufous-cheeked Nightjar).

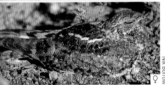

Pennant-winged Nightjar
Caprimulgus vexillarius

24–28cm A large-bodied nightjar. Both sexes have a rufous collar and no white in tail. Br. male has long white pennants; after breeding, has broad white band across black wing primaries, and drops long pennants. Female is speckled grey and brown, with no white on wings. Wings are barred rufous and black. Juv. is like female, but more rufous. **Status:** Locally common intra-African br. migrant, August to March, often on roads. **Habitat:** Developed woodland, particularly miombo. **Voice:** High-pitched cricket-like song.

African Palm Swift   *Cypsiurus parvus*

15–16cm Sexes similar. A slim, grey-brown swift with very narrow, scythe-shaped wings. Long tail is deeply forked, usually closed in flight, and appears pointed. Throat whitish with light streaking. Juv. throat greyer; rusty-brown tips to feathers and shorter outer tail feathers. **Status:** Common breeding resident in towns and gardens. Most often found near palms, such as *Borassus* and *Hyphaene* – used for breeding. **Habitat:** Various woodland types except well-developed miombo. **Voice:** A soft twittering call. Loud screeching when nesting sites disturbed.

Common Swift   *Apus apus*

16–18cm Sexes similar. A large, gregarious swift with uniform blackish-brown plumage, indistinct white throat patch and deeply forked tail. Difficult to distinguish from African Black Swift. From above, shows no contrasting secondary feathers (pale secondaries visible in African Black Swift). Juv. similar to adult but with larger white throat patch. **Status:** Common widespread Palaearctic migrant occurring October to March, often in huge flocks. **Habitat:** Most habitats. Predominantly aerial, sleeping at high altitudes. **Voice:** High-pitched scream. Mainly silent in Africa.

Little Swift

Apus affinis

12cm Sexes similar. A small, gregarious black swift with diagnostic broad white rump and square tail; also has rounded white throat patch and dark vent (see Horus and White-rumped swifts for comparison). Juv. body feathers have pale edges. **Status:** Common resident in eastern half and Mwinilunga District in west. **Habitat:** Common around cliffs and gorges where it breeds, but feeds widely in surrounding open areas. Has adapted to breeding on bridges and buildings, especially old grain silos. **Voice:** A high-pitched trilling, particularly around the nest site.

Lee Gutteridge

Horus Swift

Apus horus

14–15cm Sexes similar. A small, blackish-brown swift with broad white rump, white throat patch and a shallow fork to the tail. Similar-looking Little Swift has square-ended tail; White-rumped Swift has deeply forked tail and narrow white crescent-shaped rump patch. Juv. resembles the adult but with pale fringes to body feathers. **Status:** Resident. Mainly Luangwa Valley and Lower Zambezi. Uncommon along upper Zambezi River. **Habitat:** Sandy cliffs bordering rivers. **Voice:** Buzzy chatter.

Lee Gutteridge

White-rumped Swift

Apus caffer

14–16cm Sexes similar. A slim, gregarious swift with a white throat patch, long, deeply forked tail and a narrow crescent-shaped white rump. Tail fork may be closed during flight. (See Little and Horus swifts for comparison.) Juv. has pale edges to feathers. **Status:** Widely distributed intra-African br. migrant present August to April. **Habitat:** Occurs anywhere, often together with other swifts and swallows, particularly around rocks, bridges and houses. **Voice:** Harsh scream.

Albert Froneman

Speckled Mousebird   *Colius striatus*

30–36cm (incl. tail) Sexes similar. This mousebird is brownish overall with a black face, pale cheeks, black-and-white bill, and loosely feathered crest. There is faint barring on upper breast. Feet are reddish-brown. Juv. upper mandible greenish, no black around the face. **Status:** Resident on northern and western plateau. Avoids well-wooded parts of the north. Gregarious. Prefers wetter habitat to Red-faced Mousebird. **Habitat:** Forest edges and clearings, riparian thickets and scrub. **Voice:** Harsh, rather scratchy call.

Red-faced Mousebird   *Urocolius indicus*

32–35cm (incl. tail) Sexes similar. This mousebird has a loosely feathered crest, and long, narrow, stiff tail. Upperparts are grey with greenish sheen; underparts are buff. Red skin around eye is diagnostic. Juv. face and bill are greenish with dark tip. **Status:** Common, widely distributed resident. Gregarious and fast-flying, occurring in small flocks. **Habitat:** *Acacia* woodland, thickets, palm groves, orchards and gardens. **Voice:** Melodious three- to four-note whistled 'chivuvu', usually given in flight.

Narina Trogon   *Apaloderma narina*

30–32cm Distinctive, colourful bird. Male upperparts are metallic-green, breast and belly crimson. Bill is yellow, facial patches yellow to blue-green. Outer tail white. Female is duller with brown face and throat, pinkish-grey breast and red belly and vent. Juv. similar to female, duller with white or buff wing spots. **Status:** Common forest resident year-round, but subject to some local movement. **Habitat:** Evergreen forest including *Cryptosepalum* and *Marquesia*. Wanders into gardens and drier woodland. **Voice:** Hoarse, repetitive double hoots.

Stephanie McDougall

Glenda Sparkes

Purple Roller *Coracias naevius*

35–40cm Sexes similar. Largest roller, heavily built. Underparts are purple, heavily streaked with white. Crown and mantle are olive-green, with a broad white supercilium. Back is also olive-green, with rufous and purple wings. Bill black. Tail square ended. Juv. duller, with pale olive head and upperparts. **Status:** Intra-African migrant, mostly April to November, with some during early rains in south and west. Influxes observed in drier years. **Habitat:** Open woodland. **Voice:** Harsh crowing notes, mainly when displaying.

Racket-tailed Roller *Coracias spatulatus*

28–30cm (36cm incl. streamers) Sexes similar. This compact roller has elongated outer tail feathers with spatulate ends, a greenish-olive crown with white forehead, and broad white supercilium. The back and wings are brown with violet shoulders and primary wing coverts. Underparts are pale blue. Juv. has broad white streaks on breast, and lacks tail streamers. **Status:** Fairly common resident. **Habitat:** Well-developed mopane and miombo woodland; also *Baikiaea* forest in the west. **Voice:** Loud, high-pitched cackling notes.

Lilac-breasted Roller *Coracias caudatus*

28–30cm (37cm incl. streamers) Sexes similar. A very distinctive brightly-coloured roller with lilac throat and breast, green crown, white forehead and eye-stripe, brown back and dark blue rump. The elongated tail streamers have pointed ends (see Racket-tailed Roller). In flight, wing coverts and upper half of flight feathers are pale blue with dark blue bases. Juv. is duller with no tail streamers. **Status:** Common resident. Perches prominently. **Habitat:** Mopane and drier miombo woodland; *Baikiaea* forest in southwest. **Voice:** Variety of harsh notes mainly in display.

Sarah Solomon

European Roller
Coracias garrulus

31–32cm Sexes similar. Large roller with square tail (no extended tail streamers), pale blue head and underparts, and brown back. Wing coverts greenish-blue. In flight, black primary feathers contrast with bright blue wing coverts. Juv. duller with narrow white streaks on underparts.
Status: Widespread Palaearctic migrant occurring mainly October to May.
Habitat: Open woodland and wooded grassland. Avoids the dense miombo woodlands and *Baikiaea* forests.
Voice: Mainly silent when in Africa.

Broad-billed Roller
Eurystomus glaucurus

27–29cm Sexes similar. A compact roller with cinnamon-brown head and upperparts, and lilac underparts with purple wash. Primary and outer secondary feathers are ultramarine, with blue rump and uppertail coverts. Tail is greenish-blue with dark blue ends. Yellow bill is strong with a hooked tip; eye brown. Juv. is dull rufous-brown with brown throat, yellow bill and pale grey-blue underparts.
Status: Fairly common intra-African br. migrant, August to May. **Habitat:** Any woodland, particularly miombo and dry riparian forest. **Voice:** Harsh growling notes.

Grey-headed Kingfisher
Halcyon leucocephala

20–22cm Sexes similar. A medium-sized kingfisher with chestnut belly, white breast, grey head and all-red bill. The back and wing coverts are black; flight feathers, rump and tail are intense violet-blue. Juv. is duller with black bill and faint barring on head and breast. **Status:** Locally common intra-African migrant. Some remain to breed September to February, many on passage August to November, returning northwards April to May. **Habitat:** Most dry woodland types, mainly near water.
Voice: Loud, high-pitched chatter.

Brown-hooded Kingfisher
Halcyon albiventris

22cm Sexes similar. A medium-sized kingfisher with streaked brown head and breast, buffy collar and red bill. The rump, tail and flight feathers are blue. Male has black back and wing coverts; the female is browner. Similar Striped Kingfisher has black-red bill. Juv. is duller with a dark bill. **Status:** Locally common resident. **Habitat:** Riparian forest, thickets. Edges of evergreen and *Cryptosepalum* forest in northwest. Absent in southwest. **Voice:** A loud, piping four- or five-note trill, or a faster, equally loud trill.

Striped Kingfisher
Halcyon chelicuti

17–18cm Sexes similar. A small dryland kingfisher. The crown is heavily striped, with a broad black eye-stripe extending through the eye to the nape. Black upper and red lower mandible. Whitish neck collar. White breast and flanks have light brown streaks. Back is brown, rump and tail blue. Juv. duller, less streaked. **Status:** Common resident, usually in pairs. **Habitat:** Open woodland, wooded grassland, thickets and gardens. **Voice:** Loud, high-pitched two-note rolling trill.

Casper Badenhorst

Woodland Kingfisher
Halcyon senegalensis

23–24cm Sexes similar. Medium-sized kingfisher with grey head and blue upperparts with black 'shoulder'. Underparts whitish. Red upper mandible and black lower mandible. Legs black. Black eye patch behind eye. Juv. bill black, plumage duller. **Status:** Common intra-African br. migrant, September to May. **Habitat:** Any dry woodland. Common in *Albizia* woodland on black cotton soils, and in *Acacia* and mopane woodland in Luangwa Valley. **Voice:** Loud, high-pitched note followed by a fast trill.

Lee Gutteridge

African Pygmy Kingfisher   *Ispidina picta*

12cm Sexes similar. A small kingfisher with blue-and-black barring on crown, orange stripe between eye and crown, and lilac patch on cheeks. (See Malachite Kingfisher.) White throat, pale rufous underparts, dark blue back and rump, and blue-black wing coverts. Bill and legs red. Juv. duller with black bill. **Status:** Intra-African br. migrant, present October to April. **Habitat:** Well-developed woodland with thickets, especially miombo. Not associated with water. **Voice:** High-pitched twitter, or single 'seep' in flight.

Sarah Solomon

Malachite Kingfisher   *Corythornis cristatus*

13–14cm Sexes alike. A small kingfisher with barred turquoise-and-black crown extending down to eye (see African Pygmy Kingfisher) and erectile crest. Blue upperparts and rufous underparts; chin and neck patch white. Bill and legs red. Juv. is duller with brownish wash on underparts; bill black. **Status:** Common widespread resident. **Habitat:** Any shallow water with fringing vegetation including rivers, streams, dams and ponds. **Voice:** Very high-pitched twittering. A rapid double 'seep-seep' in flight.

Chris Krog

Half-collared Kingfisher
Alcedo semitorquata

18cm Sexes similar. An aquatic kingfisher with brilliant cobalt-blue upperparts, large white patch on sides of neck, blue half-collar on sides of breast, buffy underparts and large black bill. Base of lower mandible is reddish in female. Juv. is duller below, with mottled grey breast. **Status:** Widespread localised resident with some altitudinal movement. **Habitat:** Fast-flowing perennial rivers with well-wooded banks, particularly where there are rapids. **Voice:** Soft, very high-pitched cheeping.

Giant Kingfisher · *Megaceryle maxima*

42–46cm Largest kingfisher, with a distinctive crest and black bill. Upperparts including head are black speckled with white spots. Male breast is rufous, with white belly and throat streaked with black. Female breast is heavily streaked black and white, and belly is rufous. Juv. has black and rufous sides of neck and breast. **Status:** Widespread resident. Usually in pairs. **Habitat:** Larger rivers, lakes and dams with well-wooded banks. **Voice:** Loud and rapid chattering call 'kah-kah-kah'.

Pied Kingfisher · *Ceryle rudis*

25–28cm A large kingfisher with distinctive black-and-white plumage, and prominent black crest. Long black bill. Male has double black band across white breast; female has single broad breast band, broken in centre. Juv. has greyish-black bill, underpart feathers fringed brown. **Status:** Common resident on most waterbodies, in pairs or cooperative groups. **Habitat:** Any open stretch of water. Fishes by hovering then plunging into water. **Voice:** High-pitched single 'tshik' or equally high-pitched chattering notes.

Swallow-tailed Bee-eater · *Merops hirundineus*

22–23cm Sexes similar. A medium-sized bee-eater with diagnostic deeply forked blue tail. Broad black eye-stripe, green upperparts. Throat yellow with narrow blue necklace below; breast green, belly pale blue. Underside of wing buffy brown. Juv. duller, no necklace. **Status:** Intra-African br. migrant, from May to December. Some occur during summer rains (mid-December to March). Usually in groups. **Habitat:** Open woodland. Often seen on power lines and in eucalyptus plantations. **Voice:** Very soft twittering.

Little Bee-eater
Merops pusillus

15–17cm Sexes similar. Smallest bee-eater with green head and upperparts, and black face mask. Underparts buff with distinctive yellow throat and all-black collar. Tail square-ended or slightly forked with black tip. Central tail feathers green and outer feathers rufous. Juv. lacks collar, has greener breast. **Status:** Common resident. Usually solitary or in pairs. Parasitised by Greater Honeyguide. **Habitat:** Open woodland and grassland areas, particularly near water. **Voice:** Not very vocal; a quiet 'tsip' given irregularly.

Blue-breasted Bee-eater
Merops variegatus

18–21cm Sexes similar. Very similar to Little Bee-eater, with white cheeks and sides of neck. Collar on throat black or bluish-black; collar not very obvious in Zambian race. Juv. duller green below, lacks collar and white cheek marking not as obvious. **Status:** Resident on the dambos and floodplains in the north and west. **Habitat:** Open, permanently wet places with rank vegetation. Little Bee-eater prefers drier, more wooded areas. **Voice:** Soft, high-pitched trilling.

White-fronted Bee-eater
Merops bullockoides

23–24cm Sexes similar. Medium-sized bee-eater, named for its white forehead. Distinctive white cheeks and chin, black mask and scarlet throat. Upperparts green with deep blue rump and buffy-brown underparts. Undertail coverts blue; tail square-ended. Juv. duller overall with a green crown and orange-yellow throat. **Status:** Common resident. Parasitised by Greater Honeyguide. **Habitat:** Any woodland along most major river systems, where it nests colonially in steep banks. **Voice:** Deep, nasal sound.

Böhm's Bee-eater   *Merops boehmi*

16cm (24cm incl. streamers)
Sexes similar. A small bee-eater with green upperparts and dark chestnut head, paler chestnut throat, narrow blue cheek stripe, and very long central tail streamers (longer in male). Juv. throat yellowish; central tail streamer short or absent. **Status:** Locally common but discontinuous. Occurs solitarily or in groups of up to five pairs along the major rivers in northern and central Zambia. **Habitat:** Edges of thickets, termitaria and riverine forest along flowing rivers. **Voice:** Short series of soft, high-pitched notes; also a quiet 'tsip'.

Blue-cheeked Bee-eater *Merops persicus*

24–26cm (31cm incl. streamers)
Sexes similar. A large bee-eater with green upperparts and pale blue forehead, cheek and eyebrow. Cinnamon underwing is obvious in flight. Chin yellow, throat brown. Male eye claret-red, female eye orange-red. Tail streamers shorter in female. Juv. has no tail streamers and less blue around eye. **Status:** Palaearctic migrant present November to March. **Habitat:** Floodplains and swampy areas where it roosts. Widespread while on passage. **Voice:** Melodious trill. Pitch likened to a referee's whistle.

Olive Bee-eater   *Merops superciliosus*

24cm (30cm incl. streamers)
Sexes similar. A large bee-eater with green body, dark olive-brown crown, white supercilium and cheek stripe, and brown throat; central tail streamers longer in male. Juv. paler with short streamers, buffy-yellow chin and pale rust-coloured throat. **Status:** Intra-African migrant mainly in east, particularly the Luangwa Valley. Mainly September to early October on southwards passage, and April to May on return. **Habitat:** Open woodland. **Voice:** High-pitched, liquid trill, very similar to Blue-cheeked Bee-eater.

European Bee-eater   *Merops apiaster*

25–28cm (30cm incl. streamers)
Sexes similar. A large bee-eater with combination of rich brown crown and mantle, golden back, bright yellow throat, narrow black necklace and turquoise-blue underparts. Juv. duller, lacks tail streamers. **Status:** Palaearctic non-br. migrant present September to April. Some winter visitors from the South African breeding population may occur. **Habitat:** Most woodland habitats; absent from drier and wet extremes. **Voice:** Pleasant liquid trill often during flight. Lower note than either Blue-cheeked or Olive bee-eater.

Southern Carmine Bee-eater
Merops nubicoides

26cm (38cm incl. streamers)
Sexes similar. This large and unmistakable bee-eater has a pinkish-red body with blue crown, rump and belly; black eye mask. Very long central streamers – longer in male. Juv. duller; tail streamers absent or very short. **Status:** Gregarious common intra-African br. migrant arriving in August to September. Disperses southwards in December. **Habitat:** Open woodland; sandbanks associated with major river valleys especially the Luangwa. **Voice:** Deep, rolling 'terk-terk'.

African Hoopoe   *Upupa africana*

26–32cm Unmistakable bird. Both sexes cinnamon coloured, with black-and-white back and wings. Bill is long, thin and slightly decurved. Large black-tipped crest diagnostic, folded down to form a point at back of head, or fanned over head when alarmed or alighting. Female and juv. duller, with shorter bill and grey facial wash. **Status:** Mainly dry season breeding visitor. Some present all year. **Habitat:** Open woodland. **Voice:** Soft two- or three-note 'hoo-poo' or 'hoo-hoo-poo', repeated often.

Green Wood Hoopoe
Phoeniculus purpureus

32–40cm Sexes similar. Large hoopoe with glossy greenish-black iridescent plumage, long graduated tail with white bars in outer tail feathers, and white wingbar across middle of primaries. Long bill and short legs are bright red. Female bill is shorter and less decurved. Juv. lacks iridescent plumage; bill black. **Status:** Common widespread resident; characteristically found in small groups. **Habitat:** Any woodland, dry forest or thicket. **Voice:** Extended series of loud, cackling notes, usually given by all members of flock.

Common Scimitarbill
Rhinopomastus cyanomelas

26–30cm Sexes similar. Small and glossy blue-black bird with diagnostic long, slender, strongly decurved black bill. Legs and feet are black. In flight, shows white wingbar across primaries. Long, graduated tail has variable white spots on outer feathers. Female smaller and duller with brownish head. Juv. duller with shorter black bill. **Status:** Widespread resident, usually seen singly or in pairs. **Habitat:** Any woodland, dry forest or thicket. **Voice:** Monotonous 'weep weep weep'.

Southern Ground Hornbill
Bucorvus leadbeateri

90–110cm Sexes similar. Very large black hornbill with massive black bill and obvious red facial skin. Male has inflatable all-red skin on neck and throat; female has a violet-blue throat patch. Eyes are yellow. In flight, shows clear white wing feathers. Juv. is browner with dull yellowish face and throat turning orange with age. **Status:** Near Threatened. Widespread resident. **Habitat:** Most woodland types, grassland with thickets, dambos and montane grassland. **Voice:** Deep hooting notes in duet by dominant pair, with other group members joining in later.

Southern Red-billed Hornbill
Tockus rufirostris

40–45cm Sexes mostly similar. Smallest hornbill, black and white all over; wing coverts well spotted with white. Facial skin red, eye yellow. Long, slender, curved red bill. Male has black patch at base of lower mandible. Juv. bill shorter and pale orange; buff wing spots. **Status:** Widespread resident. **Habitat:** Particularly common in mopane woodland in the south and the Luangwa Valley, also in *Acacia* woodland. **Voice:** Loud, single- or double-noted clucking.

Southern Yellow-billed Hornbill
Tockus leucomelas

40cm Sexes similar. Larger than similar-looking Southern Red-billed Hornbill, with large yellow bill. Has pink bare skin around eyes and throat; eyes are yellow. Male has bill with distinct casque, forming a ridge along length of upper mandible. Female has shorter casque. Juv. has smaller dull yellow bill and grey eyes. **Status:** Locally common resident in south. **Habitat:** Mainly found in dry *Acacia* woodlands; also appears in some mixed woodlands. **Voice:** Long series of fast clucking notes, often with wings fanned and head held down.

Crowned Hornbill
Lophoceros alboterminatus

50–55cm Sexes similar. Large hornbill with dark brown head, upper breast and back, and white underparts. Diagnostic heavy, dark orange bill with clear yellow line at base and obvious casque. Eye yellow. Female bill smaller with shorter casque. Juv. has white edges to wing feathers and a pale yellow bill. **Status:** Common resident, usually in pairs or small groups; sometimes large post-br. congregations. **Habitat:** Tall miombo, riparian forest, edge of evergreen forest, and montane forest. **Voice:** Loud, high-pitched whistles.

African Grey Hornbill *Lophoceros nasutus*

45–50cm A medium-sized hornbill with mottled brownish-grey upperparts and white underparts; clear white stripe behind eye. Male bill black with cream patch at the base of the upper mandible and white diagonal ridges on lower mandible. Female upper mandible and casque yellow, and bill has a red tip. Juv. browner, with no casque on bill. **Status:** Common resident, with occasional large post-br. congregations. **Habitat:** Dry woodlands in south and east, including miombo, mopane, *Acacia* and *Baikiaea*. **Voice:** High-pitched piping whistles.

Pale-billed Hornbill *Lophoceros pallidirostris*

43–50cm Sexes similar. A medium-sized hornbill with light grey-brown upperparts and a broad white stripe behind the eye. Underparts white. Distinctive pale yellow bill. Eye red or red-brown; browner in female. Juv. bill without casque. **Status:** Locally common resident, mostly in small groups. **Habitat:** Well-developed miombo woodland, particularly denser and wetter more extensive stands of tall trees. **Voice:** High-pitched piping whistles similar to African Grey Hornbill, so easily overlooked.

Roy Glasspool

Trumpeter Hornbill *Bycanistes bucinator*

55–60cm Sexes similar. Large black-and-white hornbill. Heavy bill with brownish casque. Male casque runs length of bill; female casque smaller and shorter. Bare facial skin red or purple. In flight, shows white trailing edge to wings. Juv. browner with smaller casque. **Status:** Widespread resident in pairs, family groups or sometimes large congregations. **Habitat:** Well-developed riverine woodland, evergreen forest and rich miombo woodland. **Voice:** Loud, nasal 'whaaa' or braying notes; short, jerky contact call.

Lee Gutteridge

Yellow-rumped Tinkerbird
Pogoniulus bilineatus

10–12cm Sexes similar. A tiny barbet with black crown and two obvious white stripes on face. Wings with yellow edges to coverts. Back is black, rump bright yellow but not always easy to see. Juv. facial stripes absent. **Status:** A common resident in the north and northwest, solitarily or in pairs. **Habitat:** Evergreen forest and thickets, and dense riverine forest. **Voice:** A metallic four- to six-note 'pop-pop-pop-pop' with breaks in-between from the canopy.

Yellow-fronted Tinkerbird
Pogoniulus chrysoconus

11–12cm Sexes similar. Small tinkerbird with diagnostic bright yellow forehead (sometimes orange). Upperparts streaked black and white, wings with yellow margins to secondary feathers, yellow wash to pale grey underparts. Bill and legs black. Juv. similar to adult, but without yellow forehead when very young. **Status:** Common widespread resident. **Habitat:** All woodland types. **Voice:** Monotonous, loud 'pop' given repetitively from the top of a tree for long periods of time.

Miombo Pied Barbet   *Tricholaema frontata*

16–18cm Sexes similar. A barbet with black-and-white upperparts, dotted with yellow. Underparts are pale with black spots; forehead is red. The pale yellow breast and white belly are both dotted black. White throat with scaly malar stripe. Juv. lacks red forehead. **Status:** Widely distributed but sparse, near-endemic resident. **Habitat:** Miombo woodland, mixed miombo/*Baikiaea* woodland and mixed miombo/*Cryptosepalum* forests. Often found in rocky transition zones. **Voice:** Soft repetitive, ventriloquial 'hoop-hoop-hoop', like African Cuckoo.

Dan Danckwerts

Chaplin's Barbet
Lybius chaplini

19cm Sexes similar. A species endemic to Zambia. This barbet has a white head, nape, back and underparts. (Back is occasionally black in the adult.) Tail is black; black wings distinctly edged with yellow on primaries. Diagnostic red face patch above and below eye appears more vibrant when breeding. Heavy black bill, prominently notched. (Similar-looking Black-backed Barbet has red forehead, pale bill and pinkish belly.) Juv. shows varying degrees of mottled black on back; red face patch is lacking, develops with age. **Status:** Vulnerable Zambian endemic. Distribution restricted to south-central Zambia, particularly Chisamba and Choma areas, where it breeds regularly. A cooperative breeder competing with Black-collared Barbet for nest sites. Black-backed Barbet occurs further north with slight distribution overlap. **Habitat:** Edges of woodland. Almost completely restricted to areas where Sycamore Fig (*Ficus sycomorus*) is abundant, interspersed with open grassland. Sometimes forced to move from established territory due to food availability or destruction of nest sites through agricultural development. **Voice:** Either a harsh chatter or a higher-pitched trill while group displays from treetops.

white back

Stephanie McDougall

black back

Roy Glasspool

juv.   ad.

Black-collared Barbet
Lybius torquatus

20cm Sexes similar. A fairly large barbet with a bright red forehead, face and throat, and broad black collar below. Upperparts are brown, belly off-white or pale yellow. Brown flight feathers with yellow edges. Large black bill. Juv. lacks red face. **Status:** Widespread common resident in pairs or family groups. **Habitat:** Open woodland, riparian forest, grasslands with scattered thickets, suburban gardens. Avoids denser woodlands and forests. Parasitised by Lesser Honeyguide; competes with Chaplin's Barbet for nest sites. **Voice:** Loud call, starting with harsh 'skizz', then synchronised 'two-puddle' song.

Black-backed Barbet
Lybius minor

18–20cm Sexes similar. A black-and-white barbet with a bright red forehead. White underparts show pinkish wash on the belly. Black-and-white upperwings separated by a white shoulder stripe. Tail is long. Large ivory-coloured bill shows one or two 'teeth' on the sides (see Chaplin's Barbet). Juv. duller with darker bill, lacks red forehead. **Status:** Locally common resident. **Habitat:** Rich riverine habitat with *Ficus* and *Syzygium* species, evergreen forest edges, and dense thickets around termite mounds. **Voice:** A rapid but soft chatter.

Crested Barbet
Trachyphonus vaillantii

23–24cm A large multicoloured barbet with yellow face well speckled with red, and a distinctive black crest. Black breast band and back are well marked with white and yellow; belly is yellow with light red spots. Female is less brightly coloured with narrower black breast band. Juv. wings browner, with less red streaking on underparts. **Status:** Widespread common resident. **Habitat:** Most woodland types, particularly mopane and miombo. Suburban gardens. **Voice:** Loud, bubbling 'Prrrrrrrrrr', sustained for long periods (sometimes several minutes).

Lesser Honeyguide
Indicator minor

14–16cm Sexes similar. A medium-sized honeyguide with grey head, olive-green back and rump, and grey underparts. Short and stubby bill has white patch at the base, with dark malar stripes. Outer tail feathers are white with dark tips. Juv. darker below with no white patch at the base of bill, no malar stripes. **Status:** Widespread resident brood parasite. **Habitat:** Most woodland types including *Acacia*, miombo, evergreen and deciduous forest. **Voice:** A repetitive call, usually given from a regular song post, often in the canopy of a large tree.

Greater Honeyguide   *Indicator indicator*

19–20cm Largest honeyguide. Male has brown upperparts with black throat, white cheek patch and pink bill. Female is duller with white underparts, no cheek patch and no black throat; bill is black. Conspicuous white outer tail feathers in all ages and sexes. Juv. uniform brown above with yellow throat and breast, and white belly. **Status:** Common widespread resident and brood parasite. **Habitat:** All woodland types, particularly miombo and mopane. **Voice:** A loud, repetitive two-note 'Vic-turr', usually given from a prominent song post; also a chattering guiding call.

juv.

♂

Bennett's Woodpecker
Campethera bennettii

20–24cm A medium-sized woodpecker. Diagnostic heavily spotted underparts in both sexes. Male has red forehead and crown, and red moustachial stripes with white chin. Female has black forehead with white speckles, red hind crown, and brown ear patches and chin. Juv. resembles adult but with speckled crown; males with blackish malar stripe and females with the appearance of brown ear patches. **Status:** Widespread but not very common resident. **Habitat:** Light drier woodland. **Voice:** A high-pitched repeated trilling.

♀

♂

Golden-tailed Woodpecker
Campethera abingoni

20–23cm A medium-sized woodpecker with heavy black vertical streaks on off-white underparts. Belly and flanks are spotted. Male has red crown with black base to feathers, and a narrow red malar stripe with black speckles. Female has a forecrown and malar stripe speckled black and white. Juv. resembles adult, but more heavily streaked below. **Status:** Common widespread resident. **Habitat:** Miombo and other woodland types. Uncommon in evergreen forests. **Voice:** A loud, plaintive cry 'weeeea'. Occasionally rapid light drumming.

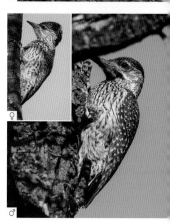

♀

♂

Dan Danckwerts

Green-backed Woodpecker
Campethera cailliautii

15–16cm Small woodpecker. Sexes similar with well-spotted underparts and no distinct malar stripes. Both sexes have red nape. Male has red forehead speckled with black; female has black forehead and crown with white spots. Juv. duller and greener above with reduced red on the nape. **Status:** Localised resident in northern half of Zambia. **Habitat:** Dense wet miombo woodland or a mixture of riparian forest and woodland. **Voice:** Rattling trill and a plaintive 'heea' call quickly repeated.

Bearded Woodpecker
Chloropicus namaquus

24–27cm The largest woodpecker with fine horizontal grey-and-white barring on breast and belly and a striking black-and-white face pattern. Male hind crown is red, female crown is black with white flecks on forehead. Juv. nape and crown are red, often mixed with black in both sexes. **Status:** Widespread resident. **Habitat:** Various mature woodland types with large trees. **Voice:** A loud series of rapid 'wik' notes; loud drumming at varying speeds from favourite trees.

Cardinal Woodpecker
Dendropicos fuscescens

14–16cm Small woodpecker with dark vertical streaks on the off-white underparts, and a barred back. Both sexes have black malar stripes and a brown forecrown. Male hind crown bright red, female crown black. Juv. duller and greyer, with red patch on the crown, and black nape. **Status:** Very common resident throughout Zambia. **Habitat:** All woodland types. **Voice:** High-pitched trilling call. Drums rapidly on both large and small branches.

Dickinson's Kestrel   *Falco dickinsoni*

27–30cm Sexes similar. A small kestrel, rather thickset with upright posture when perched. Large white-grey head. Upperparts are dark grey, rump and tail pale grey with narrow barring. Underparts vary from pale grey to brownish-grey. Eye is brown, with yellow cere, orbital ring and legs. Juv. has underparts with a brownish wash, and pale greenish-yellow cere and legs. **Status:** Resident, throughout the country, though sparse on Eastern Province plateau. **Habitat:** Lightly wooded country or grassland, favouring baobabs and palms. **Voice:** A trill 'Ki-ki-ki'.

Red-necked Falcon   *Falco chicquera*

30–36cm Sexes similar. A small falcon with deep chestnut crown and nape. Cheeks and throat are white with rufous wash on upper breast; underparts white with narrow black barring. Tail is finely barred with broad black subterminal band and white tip; upperparts of tail blue-grey with black barring. Juv. underparts have pale rufous wash and less obvious barring. **Status:** Locally common resident. **Habitat:** Woodlands and floodplains with termitaria dominated by *Borassus* and *Hyphaene* palms. **Voice:** Shrill chatter and 'Keek-keek-keek' call.

Brett Solomon

Red-footed Falcon   *Falco vespertinus*

27–32cm A small, kestrel-like falcon with red legs and feet. Male is slate-grey with deep chestnut lower belly, vent and thighs. In flight, underwings are dark. Female is grey above with rufous crown and neck, and black eye patch; pale rufous underparts are lightly streaked. Juv. similar to adult female with white cheeks and throat. **Status:** Gregarious insectivorous Palaearctic migrant, mainly from October to December while on southwards passage; some remain during rains. **Habitat:** Open woodland and grassland. **Voice:** High-pitched chatter given around roost.

Amur Falcon   *Falco amurensis*

28–30cm A small, kestrel-like falcon with grey head. Male is dark grey with chestnut vent and orange-red legs. In flight, white underwing coverts are diagnostic. Female has white cheeks and underparts with heavy black barring or spotting. Juv. similar to female with paler upperparts, and underparts with dark streaks. **Status:** Gregarious insectivorous Palaearctic migrant occurring October to April, predominantly in centre and east of Zambia. **Habitat:** Open woodland and grassland. **Voice:** High-pitched chatter when roosting.

Eurasian Hobby   *Falco subbutec*

30–35cm Sexes similar. A mid-sized, long-winged falcon with strong flight, dark cap and moustache stripe, and white supercilium, cheeks and throat. White underparts are heavily streaked with black; underwing coverts spotted white, thighs and vent rufous. Legs and cere are yellow. Juv. more heavily streaked below, with creamy-white thighs and vent. **Status:** Common, widespread non-br. Palaearctic migrant from October to April; often crepuscular. **Habitat:** Fast aerial feeder over various woodland types and in suburbia. **Voice:** Mainly silent in Africa.

Lanner Falcon   *Falco biarmicus*

39–48cm Sexes similar but female larger. A large falcon with rufous crown, narrow black moustache stripe and plain pinkish-white underparts. Blue-grey or grey-brown upperparts have a scalloped appearance. Often fans tail in flight. Juv. browner with heavy brown streaking on breast and belly; crown dull brown and paler at rear. (Juv. Peregrine has blackish crown.) **Status:** Widespread resident near cliffs and rocky gorges. **Habitat:** Very variable; open or lightly wooded country. **Voice:** Harsh scream.

Lee Gutteridge

Peregrine Falcon *Falco peregrinus*

31–40cm Sexes similar but female much larger. A large, chunky falcon with dark grey upperparts, and black head with broad black moustache stripes. Throat and cheeks white. Underparts white or pale buff with fine barring on lower breast and belly. Juv. has dark brown upperparts, with heavy black streaks on pale underparts; cere and legs grey. **Status:** Resident race mainly in eastern half of Zambia, with a scarcer migratory race. **Habitat:** Favours rocky areas, cliffs, gorges and escarpments, wandering to wetlands. **Voice:** High-pitched chatter when breeding.

Janine Scorer

Brown-necked Parrot
Poicephalus fuscicollis

32–36cm Sexes similar. Large green parrot with grey head and very large grey bill, and red shoulder and underwing patch. Males sometimes have small amount of red or orange on forecrown, females have more extensive red. Juv. head paler grey with orange-red forecrown in both sexes. **Status:** Resident in pairs with extensive local movements in post-br. flocks. Common in Luangwa Valley. **Habitat:** Varied woodlands, favouring baobabs and wild fruiting trees. **Voice:** A high-pitched shriek.

Meyer's Parrot *Poicephalus meyeri*

22–24cm Sexes similar. A medium-sized parrot, with brown head and upperparts and green or turquoise belly and rump. Obvious yellow patches on shoulders and crown. Underwing coverts yellow. Juv. has no yellow head markings and smaller shoulder patch. **Status:** Common resident in pairs or in small groups when not breeding. **Habitat:** Favours all dry woodland types including riverine, miombo and mopane. **Voice:** Strident screech.

Lilian's Lovebird   *Agapornis lilianae*

14cm Sexes similar. A familiar lovebird with reddish face, throat and upper breast. Upper- and underparts are green, wings darker green. Obvious white eye-ring and red bill. Female head and chest are paler pink. Juv. cheeks darker. **Status:** Locally common resident, forming large locally nomadic flocks post-br. **Habitat:** Mainly mopane woodland and *Acacia* and leadwood groves near water. **Voice:** Series of shrill, rather piercing notes, especially when taking flight.

Black-cheeked Lovebird
Agapornis nigrigenis

14–15cm Sexes similar. An endangered endemic lovebird with dark reddish-brown head and black cheeks, and obvious large white eye-ring. Throat and upper breast are orange, rest of body green. Bill red. Juv. similar to adult, with black marks near the base of upper mandible. **Status:** Gregarious resident, restricted to northwest of Livingstone and southern tip of Kafue National Park, mainly in small flocks. **Habitat:** Mopane woodland and the edges of *Baikiaea* forest. **Voice:** A shrill, chattering call.

African Broadbill   *Smithornis capensis*

12–14cm A tiny, stocky insectivore with a broad, rather flat bill, short tail and heavily streaked underparts. Throat is white. Male crown black, female crown dull grey or brown with black streaks. White rump feathers puff up in display. Juv. similar to adult female, with brown crown having indistinct streaks. **Status:** Locally common in suitable habitat; easily overlooked if not calling. **Habitat:** Dense riparian forests and thickets. **Voice:** Brief frog-like croak produced by vibrating outer primary feathers in display flight in early morning or late evening.

Grant Reed

African Pitta
Pitta angolensis

18–20cm Sexes similar. Unmistakable, brilliantly coloured bird with a black crown, broad buffy supercilium, bright green upperparts, and blue rump and tail coverts. Luminous blue spots on wings, pink wash to the throat and a scarlet belly. Juv. duller, with less luminous wing spots. **Status:** Uncommon intra-African br. migrant mainly from October to April. **Habitat:** Semi-deciduous thickets with dense undergrowth in Luangwa Valley and Lower Zambezi. **Voice:** A loud, frog-like single note, usually given early in the breeding season when displaying.

Roy Glasspool

Chinspot Batis
Batis molitor

12–13cm A small, common batis. Male is black and white with a broad black chest band, and grey back and crown. Female similar, but with chestnut breast band and chestnut spot on throat. Both sexes have yellow eyes. Juv. similar to female, with mottled buff upperparts. **Status:** Common widespread resident. **Habitat:** All woodland habitats, including eastern highlands and gardens. **Voice:** Loud, two- to three-syllable whistle 'weep, weep, wurp'; also harsh buzzing note.

White-crested Helmetshrike
Prionops plumatus

19–22cm Sexes similar. An unmistakable helmetshrike with black upperparts and white wingbar. Head is grey with crest of stiff or spiky feathers on the forehead and black sickle-shaped disc on the sides of the face. Eye has obvious scalloped fleshy yellow eye-ring. Juv. duller with dark brown crown and no yellow eye-ring. **Status:** Common cooperative breeding resident. Gregarious in noisy flocks. **Habitat:** Most woodland types, particularly miombo and mopane. Occurs mainly mid-stratum. **Voice:** Grating and clicking calls, usually given in group chorus.

Retz's Helmetshrike
Prionops retzii

18–21cm Sexes similar. Head and underparts are black; wings and tail chocolate-brown. Bill and legs are red, eye yellow with red fleshy eye-ring with scalloped fringe. In flight, wing shows large white patches in primary feathers; undertail coverts and tips of tail also white. Juv. is chocolate-brown with white vent; brown eye and eye-ring. **Status:** Locally common resident. Cooperative breeder. Parasitised by Thick-billed Cuckoo. **Habitat:** Well-developed woodland including riverine and deciduous forest. **Voice:** Cheerful whistled song, also a variety of grating calls in group chorus.

Grey-headed Bushshrike
Malaconotus blanchoti

24–26cm Sexes similar. Colourful shrike with massive, hooked bill. Head and nape are grey, with rest of upperparts olive-green. Distinctive white patch between base of bill and yellow eye. Underparts yellow with orange wash on the breast. Juv. head blotched grey and brown, underside less orange; eye brown to light grey. **Status:** Widespread resident. **Habitat:** Most woodland types, particularly miombo and *Acacia*. **Voice:** Various loud, often long mournful whistles; also hooting song with loud clicking, sometimes in duet.

Orange-breasted Bushshrike
Chlorophoneus sulfureopectus

18–19cm Sexes similar. A bright yellow bushshrike with green upperparts. Head grey with diagnostic yellow forehead and eyebrow, and black lores; small bill is black and eye dark brown. Underparts bright yellow with orange upper breast. Female has less orange on breast. Juv. head and face grey with light barring. **Status:** Common but shy widespread resident. **Habitat:** All types of woodland; especially common in riverine and *Acacia*. **Voice:** Soft, slow, monotonous whistle, or a faster monotonous whistle.

Brown-crowned Tchagra *Tchagra australis*

17–20cm Sexes similar. Bushshrike with brown to grey-brown crown, brown back and chestnut wings. Distinctive white eyebrow has black border above and below. Bill is black. Juv. lacks distinctive head pattern of adult, and has less chestnut wings and a horn-coloured bill. **Status:** Locally common resident apart from extreme north. **Habitat:** Rank growth throughout. Also *Acacia* savanna and gardens. **Voice:** Loud, descending series of whistles, generally given in flight while moving from one bush to another, and preceded by loud wing-fripping.

Black-crowned Tchagra *Tchagra senegalus*

20–23cm Sexes similar. The largest tchagra, has a black crown with long white eyebrow; black line through the eye separates crown from eye. Back is brown, rump grey and wings chestnut. Eye is dark brown or dark blue-grey, bill black, legs grey. Juv. has mottled black-and-brown crown, horn-coloured bill, buffy tail spots. **Status:** Common widespread resident. **Habitat:** Lower stratum of any woodland, including miombo, *Baikiaea* and mopane. **Voice:** Melodious series of three to five whistles from woodland or in display flight.

Maans Booysen

Black-backed Puffback *Dryoscopus cubla*

16–18cm A smallish bushshrike. Male head and mantle are glossy blue-black, including narrow section below the bright red eye. Back and rump white, tail black. Wing feathers black with white edges; underparts white. Female duller with greyish-white face, grey rump and grey-white underparts. In both sexes, eye colour varies from orange-red to yellow. Juv. is buff below, slate-grey above. **Status:** Very common resident; mostly single or in pairs. **Habitat:** Any forest, woodland and thicket habitat. **Voice:** Loud, distinctive double 'click-whee'; may also include growling or tearing noises.

♂

♀

Tropical Boubou
Laniarius major

19–23cm Sexes similar. A large bushshrike with glossy black upperparts and a clear white wingbar. Underparts are white with a light pink- to peach-coloured wash. Juv. bill grey-brown; duller upperpart feathers edged buff. **Status:** A rather secretive common resident. **Habitat:** Thickets, riverine and miombo woodland, seldom far from water. Present in forest edges and bracken–briar at higher elevations. **Voice:** A duet that includes a variety of musical whistles and harsh notes; also frog-like croaks and a loud growling.

Brubru
Nilaus afer

13–15cm Small black-and-white bushshrike with bright chestnut markings on the flanks. Both sexes have long, broad white eyebrow. Male has black upperparts with white down the centre, and broad white stripe on wings. Female has sooty brown upperparts with buff wing stripe. Juv. duller with less contrast; streaks on head and buffy underparts. **Status:** Common widespread resident, usually in pairs. **Habitat:** Woodland canopy throughout Zambia. **Voice:** Variety of buzzing or trilling sounds, like an old telephone ring.

White-breasted Cuckooshrike
Coracina pectoralis

25–27cm A grey-and-white cuckooshrike. Male upperparts all grey, including grey head and upper breast; underparts white. Female similar to male, but chin and upper throat white. Juv. upperparts grey with fine black barring and black spots on throat. **Status:** Localised resident with some movement to lower levels at the end of the rains. Usually in pairs and associates with bird parties. **Habitat:** Canopy of mature miombo, *Baikiaea* and mopane woodland, and *Cryptosepalum* forest. **Voice:** A weak, high-pitched series of 'tsip' notes.

Black Cuckooshrike — *Campephaga flava*

19–22cm A small cuckooshrike. Male is all-black with diagnostic orange-yellow gape. Black tail has rounded tip. A few males show yellow patch on the shoulder. Female is olive-brown above with bright yellow edges to the flight feathers and coverts, heavily barred below; no yellow gape. Juv. similar to adult female. **Status:** Common localised resident. **Habitat:** Miombo and *Acacia* woodland, dry *Cryptosepalum* forest, and edges of riverine forest. **Voice:** Very soft, high-pitched, cricket-like trill.

Maans Booysen

Magpie Shrike — *Urolestes melanoleucus*

40–50cm (incl. tail) Sexes similar. Large, long-tailed, black shrike with white scapulars forming a 'V' on the back, merging into pale grey rump. White patch in primary feathers most noticeable in flight. Female similar but with white flanks. Juv. has shorter tail and brown barring on the body feathers. **Status:** Localised resident. Gregarious, moving in loose family groups. **Habitat:** Mainly *Acacia* woodland and associated *Albizia* woodlands on black soils in the southern regions. **Voice:** Series of musical, fluty whistles.

Red-backed Shrike — *Lanius collurio*

17–18cm Male has grey head and mantle with bright russet back and black facial mask. Underparts white with pinkish wash. Female has white supercilium, brown ear coverts and fine streaking on crown. Brown chevrons on breast and flanks. Juv. similar to female, with more barring on the upperparts. **Status:** Palaearctic migrant common in October to November. Some remain during rains, with larger numbers evident on northwards passage in March to April. **Habitat:** Open woodland, particularly common in *Acacia*. Avoids denser miombo and mopane woodlands. **Voice:** Harsh 'chit chit' alarm or contact call.

Lesser Grey Shrike — *Lanius minor*

22cm Larger than Red-backed Shrike. Grey crown and back, broad black face mask, black wings and tail, and light pink-grey to white underparts. Eye is dark brown. Female is duller with greyer or brownish forehead. Juv. brownish-grey above with greyish forehead, black ear coverts and small, white distinguishing primary patch on wing. **Status:** Non-br. Palaearctic migrant occurring mainly late October to November on southwards passage; returns northwards March to April. **Habitat:** Mainly semi-arid *Acacia* savanna, mopane and secondary miombo growth. **Voice:** Harsh 'chuk'.

Stephanie McDougall

Northern Fiscal — *Lanius humeralis*

21–23cm Sexes similar. A fairly distinctive shrike with black upperparts and a grey rump with white 'V' on the back. Long black tail feathers tipped white. White primary feather patch most visible in flight. Underparts all-white. Eye dark brown, bill hooked and legs black. Juv. grey-brown, with light barring; tail tips buffy. **Status:** Formerly grouped with Southern Fiscal. Common resident, but absent from the Luangwa Valley, and scarce on Kafue Flats and the most southern areas. **Habitat:** Most open habitats, as well as gardens **Voice:** Range of whistles and harsh grating noises.

♂

Glenda Sparkes

Eurasian Golden Oriole — *Oriolus oriolus*

22–25cm The only oriole breeding in the northern hemisphere. Male is bright yellow with black wings, short yellow wingbar, short black eye-stripe and red bill. Female has greenish upperparts, white underparts with yellow flanks and undertail coverts, and lightly streaked breast. Juv. similar to female but more heavily streaked below; bill black. **Status:** Uncommon non-br. Palaearctic migrant seen mainly on passage. **Habitat:** Miombo woodland, forest patches and thickets. **Voice:** Generally silent when in Zambia, sometimes gives a liquid call, or alarm call similar to African Golden Oriole.

Paula Alçada

♀

African Golden Oriole
Oriolus auratus

20–25cm A large, bright yellow bird. Male is golden yellow with thick black line running from lores to behind eye. Wings black with yellow edges to coverts. Eye crimson and bill pink. Female is greenish-yellow above, bright yellow below, with lightly streaked underparts. Juv. greenish-yellow with black streaking on underparts; bill black. **Status:** Resident in the south, summer visitor in the north. **Habitat:** Miombo, and dry forest including *Cryptosepalum*. Montane forest outside the breeding season. **Voice:** Variety of musical notes; alarm call a harsh 'rrraaaah'.

Black-headed Oriole
Oriolus larvatus

20–24cm The only black-headed oriole in the region. Sexes similar but female duller. Head and upper breast black, eye coral-red, bill pink-red. Upper- and underparts bright yellow. Birds in northwest have greenish upperparts. Secondary feathers black with yellow edges, outer flight feathers black with white edges. Juv. has yellow streaks on head, with breast and belly streaked black, and bill black. **Status:** Very common throughout. **Habitat:** All woodland types. **Voice:** Song a melodious two- to three-note whistle; alarm call a harsh, nasal note.

Square-tailed Drongo
Dicrurus ludwigii

18–19cm Sexes similar. Smaller than the Fork-tailed Drongo. All black with metallic sheen, lightly forked tail and deep red eye. Female duller and less glossy. Red eye and strong bill helps to separate it from Southern Black Flycatcher. Juv. speckled pale grey below, with brown eye. **Status:** Common in northern half of Zambia; absent from Nyika plateau. Habitat separates it from Fork-tailed Drongo and Black Flycatcher. **Habitat:** Forests. **Voice:** Loud, ringing series of strident whistles; also gives buzzy or twanging sounds similar to Fork-tailed Drongo.

Grant Reed; Inset: Leanne Mackay

Lee Gutteridge

Fork-tailed Drongo   *Dicrurus adsimilis*

23–26cm Sexes similar. A large, noisy bird. Glossy black apart from pale inner portions of primary feathers. Tail fairly long, deeply forked. Eye dark red. (Similar-looking Black Flycatcher has dark brown eye and slight fork in the tail.) Juv. dull black with white speckles on underparts and wing coverts; eye brown. **Status:** Common widespread resident. **Habitat:** All woodland types apart from forest interior. **Voice:** Mix of loud whistles, creaking, twanging and rasping sounds; also mimics other bird calls, particularly the Pearl-spotted Owlet.

♂

Lee Gutteridge

Albert Froneman/Images of Africa

♀

African Paradise Flycatcher
Terpsiphone viridis

17–19cm (br. male 36cm) A striking bird with dark grey head and crest, cobalt-blue eye-ring and chestnut upperparts. Underparts grey. Female similar, but elongated tail feathers absent. Juv. paler. **Status:** A common intra-African br. migrant, with a race resident in north and northwest. **Habitat:** Any woodland, evergreen forest and gardens. **Voice:** Song is a loud, musical phrase; contact call a short, harsh single or double phrase.

Pied Crow   *Corvus albus*

46–50cm Sexes similar. The only white-breasted crow in the region. Glossy black with white breast and collar. Bill medium-sized and slender. (Larger White-necked Raven has heavy, white-tipped bill.) Juv. less glossy with grey tips to white feathers. **Status:** Common widespread resident. Parasitised by Great Spotted Cuckoo. **Habitat:** Most habitats; around human habitation, especially pylons and tall buildings. Avoids dense woodland and forest. **Voice:** A loud, guttural crowed 'Krhaaa'.

White-necked Raven   *Corvus albicollis*

54–56cm Sexes similar. A very large black crow with white collar and huge arched bill with white tip. (Smaller Pied Crow has slender bill.) Wing distinctly broad, tail short. Juv. upperparts brownish, rear neck flecked black, no white tip to bill. **Status:** Localised resident but wanders widely; solitary or in pairs, very occasionally joins groups. **Habitat:** Mainly along rocky hills, gorges and cliffs in northeast and east, wandering down to Livingstone. **Voice:** A loud series of croaking calls.

White-tailed Blue Flycatcher
Elminia albicauda

14cm Sexes similar. A distinctive, small flycatcher with powder-blue-grey upperparts, small crest and obvious black lores. Breast is pale grey. Long, graduated blue-grey tail with white outer feathers and tail tips. Constantly flicks tail and fans wings while feeding. Juv. slightly duller than adult, with smaller crest. **Status:** Common localised resident, often in bird parties. **Habitat:** Riparian forests, termitaria thickets and dense miombo woodland in northern half of Zambia. **Voice:** High-pitched tinny chittering.

Erie Alsworth-Elvey

White-winged Black Tit
Melaniparus leucomelas

15–16cm Sexes similar. A glossy, all-black tit with prominent, large white shoulder patch and white-edged wing feathers. Black vent. Female is duller with less glossy underparts. Juv. has brownish-black upperparts, buffy-edged wing coverts. **Status:** Widespread resident prefers higher rainfall plateau. Not normally in bird parties. **Habitat:** Light woodland and thickets on dambo edges, riparian growth; bracken–briar on Nyika. Avoids drier mopane and *Acacia* woodland. **Voice:** Various scratchy notes and a short whistle.

Nik Borrow

Southern Black Tit   *Melaniparus nige*

15–16cm A glossy, almost all-black tit, with white wing coverts with black centres. White-edged outer tail feathers. Male vent barred black and white; female grey and white. (See White-winged Black Tit.) Female upperparts less glossy, with grey underparts becoming paler grey on belly. Juv. dark brown above and greyish brown below. **Status:** Common resident in pairs, family groups and bird parties. **Habitat:** Mopane and *Acacia* woodlands in south and east; avoids well-developed miombo woodland. **Voice:** Mix of buzzy notes; musical two- to four-note call.

Rufous-bellied Tit   *Melaniparus rufiventri*

14–15cm Sexes similar. Endemic to central Africa with black head, pale yellow eye and rufous underparts. Race in parts of east has brown eyes. Western form has darker rufous underparts. Juv. duller with greyish crown and mantle, wings dark sooty brown, underparts pale. **Status:** Fairly common widespread resident, often in bird parties. **Habitat:** Various mature woodland and forest habitats including miombo, *Baikiaea* and *Cryptosephalum*. **Voice:** Mix of melodious warbling and harsh, scratchy notes.

Nik Borrow

Miombo Tit   *Melaniparus griseiventri*

14–15cm Sexes similar. Endemic to central Africa with grey back and black tail. Black wings are broadly tipped with white. Head and nape have glossy black cap, cheeks and underparts are buffy-white, and a black bib extends down to belly. Female has duller crown and throat. Juv. is like female with less extensive black bib. **Status:** Fairly common resident, often in bird parties. **Habitat:** Miombo woodlands. Also *Baikiaea* and *Cryptosepalum* forest canopy. Absent from Luangwa, Zambezi and dry *Acacia* woodlands. **Voice:** Harsh, churring notes.

Michael Buckham

Grey Penduline Tit   *Anthoscopus caroli*

8cm Sexes similar. A plain, tiny bird. Upperparts vary from grey to olive-grey in dry area race, to greenish in higher rainfall race. Forehead buffy-white, throat and breast range from white to a yellowish wash, with rest of underparts buff. Eye is brown, bill and legs grey. Juv. duller than adult. **Status:** Widespread resident except Luangwa Valley and extreme north. Family groups often roost in old weaver nests. **Habitat:** Mainly miombo and *Baikiaea* woodland; avoids mopane and *Acacia*. **Voice:** Soft, very high-pitched trill.

Eastern Nicator   *Nicator gularis*

20–23cm Sexes similar but male much larger than female. Endemic to southeast Africa, this bird is olive-green above with greyish-white underparts. Wings have distinct pale yellow spots, coverts are yellow tipped, tail has yellow edges. **Status:** Fairly common resident in low-lying valleys. A retiring, secretive species, found only in major river valleys in south and east, seldom on the escarpments, with another isolated population at Lake Tanganyika. **Habitat:** Dense riverine forest; evergreen and deciduous thickets. **Voice:** Bubbling song is loud, from deep in the canopy.

Dusky Lark   *Pinarocorys nigricans*

19–20cm Sexes similar. A large, slender lark with bold facial features, white underparts and heavily spotted breast. Dark grey above with scalloped appearance. Legs whitish. Wing flicks frequently. Female is browner, breast streaks paler. (Similar to Groundscraper Thrush, but smaller, wing coverts scalloped and absence of a light wingbar in flight diagnostic.) Juv. browner above, less heavily streaked. **Status:** Intra-African br. migrant mainly from October to April. Often seen in small flocks on burnt ground. **Habitat:** Light woodland, edges of dambos or cultivation. **Voice:** A regular 'kreep kreep'.

Rufous-naped Lark   *Mirafra africana*

16–20cm Sexes similar. A common large and stocky lark, with short, erectile rufous crest and long, strong bill appearing slightly decurved. Rufous wing panel is diagnostic. Races vary considerably in size and plumage colour. Juv. is darker above, with buff edges to feathers. **Status:** Common resident in south and southwest. Distinct isolated populations in Bangweulu, Mwinilunga and Nyika. **Habitat:** Open grassland with low bushes and termite mounds. **Voice:** A distinctive three-note whistle repeated regularly from the top of a bush or termite mound.

Flappet Lark   *Mirafra rufocinnamomea*

14–15cm Sexes similar. A fairly small and compact dark lark with a mottled, scaly pattern on upperparts. Colour varies between races from rather pale to greyish or pale brick-red. Best identified by its distinctive wing-clapping display. Juv. is darker above with pale tips to feathers. **Status:** Common resident. **Habitat:** Lightly wooded grassland, edges of miombo, mopane with sparse ground cover. Avoids treeless areas. **Voice:** Display includes loud wing-clapping and sometimes a short whistle given in flight.

Grant Reed

Red-capped Lark   *Calandrella cinerea*

14–16cm Sexes similar. A medium-sized lark, easily recognised by red patches on sides of breast and bright, unstreaked rufous cap. Crown feathers can be raised, forming a short crest. Supercilium and belly are white. Juv. is speckled above. **Status:** Intra-African br. migrant, present mainly from April to October. Most birds move north during the non-br. season. **Habitat:** Short grass on dry plains, floodplains, edges of dambos, airfields, cultivated lands and recently burnt areas. **Voice:** Mixture of trills and whistles, sometimes mimicking other birds.

Dark-capped Bulbul   *Pycnonotus tricolor*

18–20cm Sexes similar. A common bulbul with dark brown crest and head. Dark eye-ring with brown eye separates this species from very similar-looking Red-eyed Bulbul. Breast is dark brown, belly off-white, and vent and undertail coverts are bright yellow. Juv. is similar to adult but upperparts are duller with rusty wash. **Status:** Very common resident in pairs or family groups. **Habitat:** Open woodland and thickets, as well as suburban gardens. **Voice:** Song a series of cheerful liquid notes.

Little Greenbul   *Eurillas virens*

15–16cm Sexes similar. A small greenbul with grey-green upperparts, olive below. Centre of belly is pale yellow or olive, dependent on race. Southern and eastern races have a rufous tint in tail. Juv. wings are brown with russet coverts, and belly is paler. **Status:** Common yet secretive localised resident from northern Mwinilunga through to Nyika and Mafinga Mountains. **Habitat:** Evergreen, riparian forests and riverine thickets. **Voice:** Extremely vocal and noisy. Variety of chuckling notes and warbles.

Roy Glasspool

Yellow-bellied Greenbul
Chlorocichla flaviventris

20–22cm Sexes similar. A large greenbul with yellow-green upperparts, yellow below. The white, crescent-shaped eye-ring is obviously wider at the top. Eye is dark red. Juv. is similar to the adult, but with grey eye. **Status:** Common localised resident. Absent from parts of northern and western Zambia. **Habitat:** Riverine forest and thickets, semi-arid savanna woodland. Visits gardens. **Voice:** Slow series of three to five nasal notes given mid- to low-stratum.

Yellow-throated Leaflove
Atimastillas flavicollis

21–22cm Sexes similar but female smaller. A large bulbul with yellow or white throat depending on race. Pale orange eye is diagnostic. Upperparts are dark olive-brown, underparts paler grey-brown. Juv. is darker with whitish throat. **Status:** Localised resident in pairs or small parties. **Habitat:** Evergreen riparian and swamp forest edges in northern Zambia, following the course of the Zambezi River. **Voice:** Harsh chattering puppy-like 'chow chow' given by group members. Very noisy and vocal.

Roy Glasspool

Terrestrial Brownbul
Phyllastrephus terrestris

19–21cm Sexes similar but male larger. A plain brown bulbul with white chin; underparts paler than upperparts. Eye is red-brown with narrow, often-incomplete white eye-ring. **Status:** Widespread resident mainly in south and central Zambia. Moves about in small noisy groups of three to six birds. **Habitat:** Dry thickets and riparian fringing forest. **Voice:** Husky chattering call often given by group foraging through leaf litter. Also jerky repeated short alarm call given by groups from low down in undergrowth.

Lee Gutteridge

Black Saw-wing   *Psalidoprocne pristopter*

13–15cm Sexes similar. A small, all-black swallow with greenish sheen. Tail is strongly forked and outer tail feathers are elongated; female with shorter tail. Race *P. p. reichenowi* has sooty-grey underwing coverts; white in *P. p. orientalis*. Juv. is drabber with shorter tail. **Status:** Intra-African br. migrant mainly from October to May. *P. p. reichenowi* occurs west of Luangwa Valley escarpment, *P. p. orientalis* mainly on Eastern Province plateau. Some birds remain. **Habitat:** Edges of riparian and evergreen forest, and well-developed miombo woodland. **Voice:** Soft trilling call in flight.

Roy Glasspool

Grey-rumped Swallow
Pseudhirundo griseopyga

13–14cm Sexes similar. A small swallow with blue-black upperparts. Contrasting grey crown and rump are diagnostic. Underparts are white or greyish-white, tail deeply forked. Juv. has buffy-brown throat, with a scalloped appearance to upperparts, and a less deeply forked tail. **Status:** Widespread partial resident. Some populations are intra-African migrants with highest concentrations from April to October. **Habitat:** Open dry plains and edges of dambos as well as other bare or burnt ground. **Voice:** Series of soft cheeps.

Roy Glasspool

Brown-throated Martin
Riparia paludicola

12cm Sexes similar. A small, gregarious, brownish martin with off-white belly and undertail coverts. In flight, tail is all brown. Juv. has buffy scalloping on upperparts. **Status:** Resident in low-lying valleys; associated with sand cliffs along rivers. All-brown race recorded occasionally in Mwinilunga and Mafinga Mountains. **Habitat:** Mainly along major rivers in Luangwa Valley and Lower Zambezi, also Kafue and Bangweulu. **Voice:** High-pitched twittering.

Derek Keats from Johannesburg, South Africa / CC BY 2.0

Banded Martin
Riparia cincta

17cm Sexes Similar. A large martin with brown upperparts and diagnostic white eyebrow and throat; upper chest has a broad brown band. Often has narrow brown bar on vent, with rest of underparts white. Underwing coverts are white, tail brown and square-ended. Juv. has paler breast and buffy margins to upperparts. **Status:** Uncommon intra-African br. migrant with fairly wide distribution. Some birds recorded year-round. **Habitat:** Open areas such as grasslands, dambos and pastures. **Voice:** Jumble of quiet warbles and harsh notes.

Barn Swallow

Hirundo rustica

16–18cm Sexes similar but male with longer tail streamers. A swallow with metallic blue-black uperparts, rufous forehead and throat, broad blue-black breast band, and off-white to buffy underparts. Underwings and undertail coverts are off-white. Deeply forked long tail has elongated outer feathers. In flight shows white patches in the tail. Juv. is duller with buffy forehead and throat, and shorter outer tail feathers. **Status:** Very widespread Palaearctic migrant October to March. **Habitat:** All open habitats; avoids forest. **Voice:** High-pitched twittering.

White-throated Swallow
Hirundo albigularis

14–17cm Sexes similar. Glossy, blue-backed swallow with white throat, complete or partial blue breast band and rufous forecrown. Underparts are dull white. Fairly deeply forked tail shows white spots. Juv. is duller with brown breast band and no rufous forehead. **Status:** Intra-African migrant mainly between March and December. **Habitat:** Floodplains and open grasslands on the plateau, particularly Bangweulu and Kafue Flats. **Voice:** Soft, high-pitched warble.

Wire-tailed Swallow

Hirundo smithii

13–17cm Sexes similar. A small, fast and agile swallow with glossy blue uperparts and rufous crown. Underparts are totally white, with black vent band. Long, wire-like outer tail feathers are shorter in the female. (Larger White-throated Swallow has rufous forehead and blue-black breast band.) Juv. is duller with pale crown and shorter tail. **Status:** Common widespread resident, usually in pairs. **Habitat:** Always associated with waterbodies, including large rivers, often around jetties and boats. **Voice:** Mix of soft warbles and high-pitched chitters.

Rock Martin   *Ptyonoprogne fuligula*

14–16cm Sexes similar. A stocky, dark brown martin with a pinkish-rust wash to the throat. Tail is square, with distinguishing white spots on the inner webs visible above and below in flight. (See similar-looking Brown-throated Martin.) Juv. has buffy tips to upperpart feathers. **Status:** Common resident. **Habitat:** Mountains, cliffs, gorges and even tall buildings in towns. **Voice:** Not very vocal. Harsh growling call given in flight.

Common House Martin   *Delichon urbicum*

13–14cm Sexes similar. A stocky, swallow-like martin with blue crown and back, white rump and shallow-forked tail. Underparts are white. Non-br. birds have a brownish wash on the face, breast and flanks. White feathering on legs. Similar Grey-rumped Swallow has pale-grey rump and crown, and deeply forked tail. Juv. has grey-brown upperparts and off-white rump. **Status:** Palaearctic migrant mainly from October to mid-April. Some birds overwinter. **Habitat:** Widespread favouring hilly country. **Voice:** Soft, harsh warbles.

Andreas Trepte / CC BY-SA

Lesser Striped Swallow
Cecropis abyssinica

15–19cm Sexes similar. A small swallow with rufous crown, ear coverts and rump; heavily streaked white underparts are diagnostic. Upperparts are glossy dark blue. Deeply forked tail has elongated outer feathers; female tail feathers are shorter. Juv. is duller with brownish edges to wing coverts, buff-washed breast and shorter tail. **Status:** Common widespread resident, mostly in pairs. **Habitat:** Open savanna and well-wooded areas along rivers. **Voice:** Various squeaky and nasal notes.

Casper Badenhorst

Red-breasted Swallow *Cecropis semirufa*

22–24cm Sexes similar. A large swallow with blue-black crown and upperparts, rufous throat and breast, dark blue ear coverts, and rufous underparts and rump. Underwing coverts are pale rufous. (Mosque Swallow has white ear coverts and whitish underwing coverts.) Elongated outer tail feathers form long streamers. Juv. has pale rufous chin and throat, brownish upperparts and shorter tail streamers. **Status:** Intra-African br. migrant, some present year-round. **Habitat:** Open and wooded grassland; often near aardvark holes and road culverts. **Voice:** Soft twitter.

Casper Badenhorst

Mosque Swallow *Cecropis senegalensis*

22–24cm Sexes similar. The largest swallow, with glossy blue-black back, crown and nape. Collar is rufous, face and throat are white, underparts rufous and ear coverts white. Underwing coverts are pale buff or white. Outer tail feathers are elongated. (Similar Red-breasted Swallow has rufous throat and breast, dark blue ear coverts and buffy underwing coverts.) **Status:** Locally common resident but with some local movement. Pairs often perch on power lines. **Habitat:** Open woodland; associated with baobabs. **Voice:** Harsh chirp and nasal whistle.

Lee Gutteridge

Moustached Grass Warbler
Melocichla mentalis

18–20cm Sexes similar. A large grass warbler with strong bill and long, broad tail with rounded tip. Forehead is rufous and throat white, with prominent black malar stripe (the 'moustache'). Eye varies from pale yellow to reddish orange. Juv. is duller with brown crown, dark eye and no malar stripe. **Status:** Locally common resident in north and northeast, and westwards to northwest. **Habitat:** Long, rank grass, particularly in floodplains and dambos; also grassy edges of woodland and old cultivated lands. **Voice:** Repetitive, bubbling song.

Long-billed Crombec   *Sylvietta rufescens*

11cm Sexes similar. A small warbler with long, slightly curved bill; appears completely tailless. Upperparts are grey and face whitish with a pale supercilium and a dark eye-stripe behind the eye. Underparts are buff coloured. Juv. is similar to adult. **Status:** Common widespread resident in pairs or family groups. **Habitat:** Drier woodlands and thickets including mopane and *Acacia* scrub. Avoids well-developed miombo woodland. **Voice:** Repeated loud, trilling song.

Red-capped Crombec   *Sylvietta ruficapilla*

10–11cm Sexes similar. Crombec with pale grey upperparts. Name confusing as common race *S. r. chubbi* has grey crown, chestnut ear coverts, white throat and chestnut breast band. Race *S. r. gephra* found in northwest to north has grey forehead and rich chestnut crown and nape. Juv. is similar to adult but paler below. **Status:** Fairly common resident locally; joins mixed bird parties. **Habitat:** Canopy of miombo woodland and *Cryptosepalum* forest. **Voice:** Loud, trilling song.

Maans Booysen

Race *S. r. gephra*

Grant Reed

Race *S. r. chubbi*

Livingstone's Flycatcher
Erythrocercus livingstonei

10–12cm Sexes similar. A small flycatcher. The long, rufous tail is regularly fanned with small black spots towards end of tail feathers. Head is grey, back greenish-yellow, chin and throat are grey-white; rest of underparts are bright yellow. Juv. lacks tail spots. **Status:** Restricted to low-lying areas, where fairly common. Pairs or family groups occur mid- to top stratum. **Habitat:** Thickets in deciduous and riverine forest, also evergreen miombo woodland. **Voice:** Series of short, warbling notes.

Roy Glasspool

Willow Warbler   *Phylloscopus trochilus*

11–12cm Sexes similar. A small, slender warbler with a thin, spiky bill and long, whitish eyebrow. Long tail is slightly forked or notched. Legs are pinkish brown. (Icterine Warbler has blue-grey legs.) Upperparts vary from greenish-yellow to brown, underparts are yellow to almost white depending on race. Juv. is yellower below. **Status:** Very abundant Palaearctic migrant occurring October to March. **Habitat:** All open woodland types, edges of evergreen forests, plantations and gardens. **Voice:** Call is a soft two-note 'hooeet'; the song a melodious warbling.

Greater Swamp Warbler
Acrocephalus rufescens

16–18cm Sexes similar. A large warbler with dark grey-brown upperparts, plain face, obvious short, rounded wings and greyish-white underparts. Often raises crest when singing. Inconspicuous dark feather shaft streaks on throat. **Status:** Locally common resident. Very shy and secretive, best located by deep, throaty song. **Habitat:** Permanent swamps and marshes with stands of papyrus and other reeds. **Voice:** Loud, deep and short chuckling phrases with harsher notes in-between. (See Lesser Swamp Warbler.)

Lesser Swamp Warbler
Acrocephalus gracilirostris

17–18cm Sexes similar. A robustly built warbler with drab brown upperparts and paler underparts, has a pronounced white eye-stripe, and white face and underparts with no streaking. Wings are short and rounded. Pale brown rump is visible in flight. Bill is long, and legs are dark grey. (Little Rush Warbler has pink legs.) Juv. is similar to adult but with warmer brown upperparts and greyish washed underparts. **Status:** Common widespread resident. **Habitat:** Reeds and bulrushes over any waterbody. **Voice:** Rich, melodious notes, usually given from within reedbeds.

Great Reed Warbler
Acrocephalus arundinaceus

19–20cm Sexes similar. A large warbler with a long, sturdy bill, unstreaked and warm-toned olive-brown upperparts, broad buffy eyebrow, dark lores and buffy underparts; often faint streaking on throat. Juv. is brighter than adult, with warm rusty brown above and buff below. **Status:** Palaearctic migrant, mainly December to March. **Habitat:** Reedbeds, rank vegetation and thickets near water; also in thickets in gardens. **Voice:** Loud series of grating and high-pitched, rather tinny notes.

Nik Borrow

Sedge Warbler
Acrocephalus schoenobaenus

12–13cm Sexes similar. A slender warbler with a streaked crown and mantle, and broad white eyebrow with black band above. Lower back and rump are russet. Tail is dark brown, short and rounded, wings are long, legs greyish-brown. Juv. is more buff coloured, yellow below. **Status:** Common Palaearctic migrant mainly December to April; very few records from Luangwa Valley. **Habitat:** Marshy areas with thickets of grasses or reeds. **Voice:** Sustained grating, chattering notes; contact call a singular 'tuck'.

Nik Borrow

African Reed Warbler
Acrocephalus baeticatus

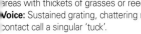

12–13cm Sexes similar. A small warbler with warm brown upperparts and rufous rump. Underparts and throat are whitish with buff wash on breast. Eye is dark brown; bill is dark brown above, yellowish below. Wing does not extend beyond rump. Juv. is brighter and more rust coloured. **Status:** Locally common breeding resident; non-br. visitors from southern Africa in winter months. **Habitat:** Reedbeds and marshes in south and east. **Voice:** Rapid rambling series of grating and churring notes.

Maans Booysen

African Yellow Warbler
Iduna natalensis

13–15cm Sexes similar. A distinctive medium-sized warbler with yellowish-olive-brown upperparts including head and neck; underparts are bright yellow with a light olive wash on side of the breast, belly and flanks. Eye is brown, bill black above, horn below; legs are steel-grey. Juv. is buff-coloured. **Status:** Present year-round; dry-season visitor in Kafue Flats. Absent from the west. **Habitat:** Rank grass along streams and dams, marsh edges; bracken–briar in eastern highlands. **Voice:** Melodious trill; also repetitive, four-to five-note series of harsh warbles.

Lee Gutteridge

Icterine Warbler
Hippolais icterina

13–14cm Sexes similar. This warbler has two colour morphs: yellow and grey. Common yellow form is greyish-green above with lemon-yellow underparts. Scarcer grey form is grey-brown above, creamy-white below. Head is large with peaked crown; orange base to bill. (See Willow Warbler for comparison.) Juv. is duller with brownish tinge to upperparts, whiter below. **Status:** Fairly common Palaearctic visitor, November to April. **Habitat:** Mainly canopy of *Acacia* woodland, sometimes other woodland types. **Voice:** Varied mix of harsh notes and melodious whistles.

Little Rush Warbler
Bradypterus baboecala

14–15cm Sexes similar. A dark brown warbler with broad, heavy, brown, rounded tail. Underparts are paler brown, undertail coverts dull rufous. May show faint streaks on throat. Bill is black with grey base; legs pink. Juv. has yellow tinge to underparts. **Status:** Common widespread resident. **Habitat:** Permanent swamps where it creeps around, mouse-like, in reedbeds or sedges. **Voice:** Song an important aid to identification: series of accelerating trills often accompanied by wing-fripping.

Fan-tailed Grassbird
Schoenicola brevirostris

16–18cm Sexes similar. A large warbler with small head and bill, and long, broad, graduated black tail. Upperparts rich brown, underparts grey-white with greyish-brown undertail coverts. Juv. has yellow wash to underparts and shorter, narrower tail. **Status:** Common localised resident in northwest and north, down to Luangwa Valley escarpment. Sparse in Western, Central and Southern provinces. **Habitat:** Long, rank grass in dambos and montane areas. **Voice:** Soft, high-pitched, single note.

Erle Alsworth-Elvey

Red-faced Cisticola   *Cisticola erythrops*

13–15cm Sexes similar. A plain-backed cisticola. Non-br. birds have browner upperparts and crown, and olive wash on nape. Rufous face is only present in breeding adult. Tail has dark subterminal band with buffy-grey tips. Juv. is browner. **Status:** Absent from the west, otherwise common resident countrywide. **Habitat:** Long, rank grass along streams and edges of marshes; also in lush suburbia. **Voice:** Ticking notes followed by loud, strident ringing notes that increase in volume.

Lee Gutteridge

Trilling Cisticola   *Cisticola woosnami*

13–14cm A plain-backed cisticola with dull rufous crown. Upperparts are dark reddish-brown, underparts are pale buff. Bill is stout. Br. male has greyer upperparts. Female is smaller than male, paler above and more buffy below. Juv. is more rufous above and buffy below. **Status:** Locally common on northwestern and northern plateau. **Habitat:** Wet miombo woodland with long grass. **Voice:** Long, ringing trill that increases in intensity and volume.

Lee Gutteridge

Rattling Cisticola
Cisticola chiniana

12–15cm Sexes similar but male larger than female. A large, robust cisticola. Upperparts are brownish with grey-brown streaks, crown is rufous-brown, underparts are buffy. Tail is well spotted. Strong, decurved bill. Br. male shows black gape when calling. Juv. is similar to adult. **Status:** Common widespread resident, though less so in northwestern and western parts; absent from extreme north. **Habitat:** Woodland savannas. **Voice:** Loud phrase of two to four 'cheers' followed by rattling trill, given from top of a bush or tree.

Chirping Cisticola
Cisticola pipiens

12–14cm Sexes similar. A plain, medium-sized cisticola with grey-and-black streaks on back. Tail is long, broad and heavy. Crown is dull brown and wing panel less visible than those of other wetland cisticolas. Juv. is whiter on face, with buff flanks. **Status:** Widely distributed in wetlands in north and west, and southwest. **Habitat:** Tall reedbeds and papyrus growing in permanent water. **Voice:** Song is two to three chipping notes then a buzzy trill. Short display flight by male while calling.

Lee Gutteridge

Stout Cisticola
Cisticola robustus

13–16cm Sexes similar but female smaller. A large, robust cisticola with heavy bill, rufous crown and nape, and boldly striped upperparts. Mwinilunga birds have very dark upperparts. (Croaking Cisticola has brown crown and nape.) Juv. is less heavily streaked above, with yellow wash to underparts. **Status:** Mwinilunga area, also relatively common in northeast. **Habitat:** Tall grass in the more extensive, moist dambos. **Voice:** Song a rapid, buzzy series of notes; call a harsh 'chip-chip-chip'

Lee Gutteridge

Croaking Cisticola — *Cisticola natalensis*

13–17cm Sexes similar but female smaller. A large cisticola with very heavy, decurved bill. Upperparts are streaked dark grey-brown in the br. male; paler in winter. Bill black in br. male, brown in female and non-br. male. Non-br. bird has paler plumage. Juv. is duller with yellow wash to underparts. **Status:** Common localised resident. **Habitat:** Moist open dambos and floodplain grassland with scattered bushes and trees. **Voice:** Loud, croaking call from a prominent perch or during a low circular display flight. A steady, ticking alarm call.

Dan Danckwerts

Short-winged Cisticola — *Cisticola brachypterus*

10–11cm Sexes similar. A small, plain cisticola with brown crown and unstreaked upperparts, and dark brown subterminal band with pale tip to tail. Non-br. male is mottled above, especially on crown; underparts are darker buffy. (Similar Neddicky has rufous crown and wing panel.) Juv. is paler with yellow wash. **Status:** Locally common over most of the plateau. **Habitat:** Zone between woodland and grassland; cultivated areas. **Voice:** Soft series of high-pitched notes either given from top of a tree or in flight.

Stephanie McDougall

Neddicky — *Cisticola fulvicapilla*

10–11cm Sexes similar. A small, plain, dark-backed cisticola with rufous crown. (Short-winged Cisticola has brown crown.) Medium-length tail has no subterminal spots. (Larger Lazy Cisticola has tail spots and repeatedly elevates tail like prinia.) Juv. is duller. **Status:** Common widespread resident in the drier half of the country. **Habitat:** All levels in various woodland types, especially the understorey of broad-leaved woodland. **Voice:** High-pitched 'seep-seep-seep-seep' that may be repeated for long periods, often calling from treetops. Rapid ratchet alarm call.

Maans Booysen

Zitting Cisticola
Cisticola juncidis

10–11cm Sexes similar. Fairly large cloudscraping cisticola with streaked upperparts and short, dark brown, fan-shaped tail with dark subterminal band and white tips. Non-br. bird is browner overall with heavy black streaking on crown. (Desert Cisticola crown is streaked brown.) Juv. has yellowish wash on upper and lower parts. **Status:** Widespread localised resident. Absent from northwest. **Habitat:** Moist grassland avoiding tall grass. Also cultivated lands and airfields. Absent from high montane grasslands. **Voice:** Regular 'zit-zit-zit' call in bouncing flight or when perched.

Desert Cisticola
Cisticola aridula

10–11cm Sexes similar. Small cloudscraping cisticola with medium-length rounded tail and streaked back. Brown streaking on crown. (Zitting Cisticola crown is streaked black.) Rump is grey-brown with fine streaks. Plumage is generally paler than other cloudscrapers. Subterminal dark band on tail is indistinct. Juv. has yellow wash overall. **Status:** Locally common resident in west and south, Bangweulu Swamps and Eastern Province plateau. **Habitat:** Dry, short grass and bare locations. **Voice:** High-pitched 'si-si-si', often with audible wing snaps.

Pale-crowned Cisticola
Cisticola cinnamomeus

10cm A localised cisticola. Br. male has unstreaked buffy-white crown and black mask or lores. Tail is blackish with white tips. Both sexes have streaked upperparts. Non-br. adults have a streaked crown, making it very difficult to distinguish from other non-br. cloudscrapers. Juv. underparts have pale yellow wash. **Status:** Locally common resident. **Habitat:** Short, wet grasslands in dambos and marshes. **Voice:** Monotonous, high-pitched, somewhat squeaky sound in the sky or from a grassland perch. It does not snap wings in descent.

Tawny-flanked Prinia   *Prinia subflava*

12–14cm Sexes similar. A mainly brown prinia with a distinct white eyebrow contrasting with darker eye-stripe, reddish eyes, tawny flanks and rufous edges to wings. Long, graduated tail constantly cocked and swivelled round is diagnostic. Juv. eye is dark, underparts lemon washed. **Status:** Very common widespread resident in pairs or small family groups. **Habitat:** All habitats with long grass and disturbed or tangled vegetation. **Voice:** High-pitched cheeping call; also a monotonous ticking.

Lee Guttridge

Yellow-breasted Apalis   *Apalis flavida*

12–13cm Sexes similar. The only apalis with a yellow breast and no breast band. Upperparts are green, face and crown grey, throat white, breast yellow and belly white. Eye is dark red. Males have black spot below yellow breast, sometimes absent when not breeding. Juv. is duller green above with paler yellow breast. **Status:** Widespread localised resident in family groups, pairs or mixed bird parties; often gleaning in treetops. **Habitat:** Riparian forest, woodland and thickets. **Voice:** Call is repetitive; male a grating 'krrik krrik', female responds 'jee jee jee'.

♀
♂

Brown-headed Apalis   *Apalis alticola*

12cm Sexes similar. This apalis has grey-brown upperparts, a dark brown head and creamy-white underparts. Grey tail with white tips to outer tail feathers is diagnostic. Legs are pink. Male eye is red, female eye pale orange-yellow. Juv. is olive-brown above, yellowish below. **Status:** Uncommon resident restricted to the northwest, and northern and northeastern highlands; usually in pairs or family groups. **Habitat:** Larger patches of mature, tall, evergreen montane, and riverine and mushitu swamp forests; also well-developed evergreen thickets. **Voice:** Repetitive 'chik chik' in duet.

Grant Reed

Grey-backed Camaroptera
Camaroptera brevicaudata

12–13cm Sexes similar. A small, compact bird. Head, mantle and back are grey when breeding. Throat and upper breast are pale grey, lower breast and belly are buffy-white, wings olive-green. Non-br. plumage is paler and browner. Juv. has olive-brown upperparts lightly streaked below. **Status:** Very common widespread resident. **Habitat:** Thickets throughout, but absent west of the Muchinga Mountains and parts of North-Western Province. **Voice:** Very vocal species; loud, repetitive clicking and bleating alarm call.

Stierling's Wren-Warbler
Calamonastes stierlingi

13cm Sexes similar. A small, skulking bird with rufous-brown upperparts, white spots on wings, black-and-white speckled lores, and dark barring on throat and breast, becoming broader on belly and flanks. Eye is red-brown, bill black, legs light brown. Juv. has yellow wash on underparts and a brown bill. **Status:** Fairly common resident in the southern half. **Habitat:** Woodland with grassy understorey and thickets. **Voice:** Repetitive, distant three- to four-note 'tirrup tirrup'.

Yellow-bellied Eremomela
Eremomela icteropygialis

9–10cm Sexes similar. A pale eremomela with a short tail and grey upperparts. Chin, throat and breast are grey-white, lower belly and vent yellow, and softer yellow in birds from southern region. Red-brown eyes with pale, narrow supercilium and dark eye-stripe. Juv. has duller yellow underparts. **Status:** Common woodland species; single or in family groups, joins bird parties. **Habitat:** Various open woodlands, particularly miombo and mixed *Acacia–Combretum*. Avoids extremely wet miombo, scarce in low-lying major valleys. **Voice:** A short, musical warble.

Lee Gutteridge

Green-capped Eremomela
Eremomela scotops

11–12cm Sexes similar. A striking eremomela with greenish-grey upperparts. Crown is pale grey, yellow in br. male. Upper breast is yellow, with underparts fading to paler yellow or sometimes white. Pale yellow eye with a narrow red eye-ring is diagnostic. Juv. is paler. **Status:** Very common woodland species. **Habitat:** Miombo and *Baikiaea* woodland, and edges of *Cryptosepalum* forest. **Voice:** High-pitched 'tillup' by a single bird, or more often a repetitive chatter by the flock calling together.

Burnt-necked Eremomela
Eremomela usticollis

10–11cm Sexes similar. An ashy-grey eremomela with creamy-yellow underparts and bright cream eye. The 'burnt neck' brown throat bar is often inconspicuous and varies in size, sometimes absent in winter. Rusty tinge across cheeks varies and not always visible. Juv. lacks rusty cheeks and brown throat bar. **Status:** Localised resident in small family groups. **Habitat:** Stands of tall *Acacia* and Winterthorn (*Faidherbia albida*) mainly in canopy. **Voice:** A very high-pitched, rapid trill given by the various members of the flock.

Lee Gutteridge

Arrow-marked Babbler *Turdoides jardineii*

25–28cm Sexes similar. A widespread babbler with dull brown upperparts and lighter brown underparts. Feathers on throat and breast are diagnostically arrow-shaped with white tips. Centre of eye is yellow, outside is orange-red. Juv. is similar to adult but with brown eyes; lacks arrow-shaped feathers. **Status:** Common, gregarious, cooperative breeding resident; scarce in far west. Parasitised by Levaillant's Cuckoo. **Habitat:** Most woodland, thickets and rank grass. Avoids short-grass woodlands without thickets. **Voice:** Raucous chatter in chorus by various members of the flock, rising then falling away.

Roy Glasspool

Hartlaub's Babbler   *Turdoides hartlaubii*

24–26cm Sexes similar. This brownish babbler's white rump and scalloped feathers on head, neck and throat separate it from similar Arrow-marked Babbler. Juv. is similar to adult with paler throat. **Status:** Resident cooperative breeder in most of Zambia west of the Luangwa Valley escarpment. Absent from much of the east and southeast. Parasitised by Levaillant's Cuckoo. **Habitat:** Papyrus and reed swamps with termitaria thickets; also large, permanently wet dambos with fringing riparian vegetation. **Voice:** Noisy, rather nasal chatter, often given in chorus.

Nik Borrow

African Yellow White-eye
Zosterops senegalensis

11–12cm Sexes similar. A bright white-eye with yellowish-green upperparts and bright yellow underparts. White eye-ring is diagnostic. Juv. is paler below. **Status:** Common resident throughout much of Zambia. Scarce in the far north. Occurs in small groups, mixes with bird parties. Parasitised by Green-backed Honeybird. **Habitat:** Well-developed miombo woodland, evergreen forest, *Cryptosepalum* forest, thickets, riparian vegetation and suburbia. **Voice:** A soft series of pleasant warbles or whistling notes.

©Paul van Giersbergen

Yellow-bellied Hyliota   *Hyliota flavigaster*

11–12cm A small bird, similar to Southern Hyliota. Male upperparts are metallic blue-black, underparts yellow-orange. Large white wing panel extends to secondary feathers. (Southern Hyliota has smaller wing panel.) Female is dark grey-brown above and white wingbar is less marked. Juv. is similar to adult female, but lightly barred on back. **Status:** Common resident in suitable habitat. Occurs in pairs in bird parties, often together with Southern Hyliota. **Habitat:** Canopy of miombo woodland; absent from *Cryptosepalum* forest. **Voice:** High-pitched chitter.

Southern Hyliota *Hyliota australis*

11–13cm Male has matt-black upperparts; white wingbar is restricted to greater wing coverts. (See Yellow-bellied Hyliota.) Underparts, throat and chest are orange-yellow, belly is pale yellow. Female is duller with deep brown upperparts and pale yellow underparts. Juv. is similar to adult female but duller. **Status:** Common localised resident; absent from extreme west, north and east; occasionally in Luangwa Valley. Occurs in pairs in bird parties. **Habitat:** Miombo woodland canopy; uncommon in *Cryptosepalum* forest. **Voice:** High-pitched chittering notes.

Piet Zwanniken

African Spotted Creeper *Salpornis salvadori*

14–15cm Sexes similar. A small, creeping bird with a light brown body covered with distinctive white spots and bars. Decurved bill is long and slender. Juv. is duller, otherwise similar to adult. **Status:** Localised resident, uncommon on the plateau in northern and eastern Zambia and in west towards the Zambezi. Mostly absent from low-lying valleys. Joins bird parties when not breeding. **Habitat:** Tall, well-developed undisturbed miombo woodland, favouring stands of rough-barked species such as *Brachystegia spiciformis*. **Voice:** Very high-pitched wispy call.

Michael Buckham

Wattled Starling *Creatophora cinerea*

21cm Compact starling with pale grey upperparts, white rump, and black wing and tail feathers. Br. male has bright yellow hind crown and large black wattles, vestigial in non-br. male. Female has dark brown wing, and grey tail feathers and upperwing coverts. Bill is horn-coloured in both sexes. Juv. is like female, bill initially yellow. **Status:** Highly nomadic; flocks may appear anywhere, often around grazers. **Habitat:** Open woodland or grasslands. **Voice:** Song various whistling notes; alarm call a rasping note.

♂ ♀

Greater Blue-eared Starling
Lamprotornis chalybaeus

21–24cm Sexes similar. A fairly large starling with glossy greenish-blue upperparts, dark blue ear coverts, and royal-blue flanks and belly. Eyes are yellow (see Miombo Blue-eared Starling), bill and legs black. Juv. is duller with underlying brown plumage and brown eye. **Status:** Common resident. **Habitat:** Open woodland habitats, especially *Acacia*, short grass and bare ground. Absent in northwest and parts of Northern Province. **Voice:** Jumble of warbles and whistles; also diagnostic 'squeer' call.

juv.

ad.

Piet Zwanikken

Miombo Blue-eared Starling
Lamprotornis elisabeth

18cm Sexes similar. A smaller starling with glossy blue-green upperparts, narrow dark blue ear coverts, and glossy blue-green underparts with magenta flanks and belly. Eye is orange-yellow (see Greater Blue-eared Starling), bill and legs are black. Diagnostic juv. underparts are mottled chestnut and magenta. **Status:** Common localised resident, favours miombo woodlands, moving in small or sometimes large loose feeding flocks. Roosts communally. **Habitat:** Miombo woodland. **Voice:** Song a melodious series of whistles.

Meves's Starling   *Lamprotornis mevesi*

32–34cm Sexes similar. A medium-sized starling with long, strongly graduated tail and slender body. Ear coverts are black. Upperparts are glossy blue-green and underparts violet. Eye, bill and legs are dark. Juv. underparts are matt black, tail is shorter than in adult. **Status:** Common resident in Luangwa and Lower Zambezi valleys and much of the south. Often forms large wintering roosting flocks. **Habitat:** Mopane and *Acacia* woodland, particularly tall woodland, and seasonally flooded areas. **Voice:** Grating whistle.

Violet-backed Starling
Cinnyricinclus leucogaster

16–18cm Male is unmistakable with iridescent violet head, upperparts, throat and upper breast. Underparts are pure white. Eyes are brown with yellow rim, bill and legs are black. Female is chestnut-brown above and white below, with heavy streaking. Juv. has broad rufous edges to body feathers, dark brown eye and brown legs. **Status:** Common intra-African br. migrant September to March, some remain year-round. **Habitat:** Common in miombo woodland and deciduous and evergreen forest. **Voice:** Soft, short whistles.

Red-winged Starling   *Onychognathus morio*

27–30cm A large starling. Male is all-black with fairly long, graduated tail. Rufous wing-patch is strikingly visible in flight. Eye is dark red, bill and legs black. Female head and throat are grey; upper breast streaked with black. Juv. is like male with dull black plumage and dark brown eye. **Status:** Locally common resident. Usually in pairs when breeding; congregates in small non-br. flocks. **Habitat:** Rocky hills and gorges on major rivers in eastern part of country. **Voice:** Various musical whistling notes.

Yellow-billed Oxpecker
Buphagus africanus

19–21cm Sexes similar. Slightly larger but easily confused with Red-billed Oxpecker. Diagnostic pale brown rump contrasts with darker brown upperparts. Easily seen in the field. Bill is yellow with red tip, no yellow ring around red eye. Juv. is darker with brown eye and bill. **Status:** Resident in areas with large wildlife. Under threat from use of non-oxpecker-friendly cattle dip in areas adjacent to national parks. **Habitat:** Wooded areas with host animals present. **Voice:** Hissing call interspersed with clicks.

Red-billed Oxpecker
Buphagus erythrorhynchus

19–21cm Sexes similar. Slightly smaller than Yellow-billed Oxpecker with uniform brown upperparts and no pale rump (see Yellow-billed Oxpecker); underparts are buff. Eye is red with yellow eye-ring, bill is red. Juv. has black bill and brown eye. **Status:** Resident in large game areas with some wandering. Usually in family groups. Under threat from use of non-oxpecker friendly cattle dip in areas adjacent to national parks. **Habitat:** Open woodland where host animals occur. **Voice:** Harsh hissing call.

Groundscraper Thrush   *Turdus litsitsirupa*

22–24cm Sexes similar. A medium-sized upright thrush with grey upperparts, black-and-white streaks on sides of face, and white underparts with black, teardrop-shaped spots on breast and belly. Often wing-flicks. Prominent orange wing panel is obvious in flight. Juv. is similar with buff spotting above and buffy tinge below. **Status:** Widespread but generally uncommon, mostly in pairs or family groups. **Habitat:** Tall miombo, *Burkea* and mixed woodland with open understorey; parks and lawns in suburbia. **Voice:** Various repeated, slow whistles.

African Thrush   *Turdus pelios*

21–23cm Sexes similar. Widespread thrush. Zambian race *T. p. stormsi* has dark brownish-olive upperparts, dark orange underparts, buffish streaked throat, olive wash on breast, and pale vent. Bill is yellow, legs flesh brown. (Similar looking Kurrichane Thrush has distinct black-and-white throat markings and occupies different habitat.) Juv. is browner with light grey spots on breast and belly. **Status:** Common localised resident occurring singly or in pairs. **Habitat:** Evergreen forests in northwest and northern Zambia. **Voice:** Loud series of melodious notes.

Nik Borrow

Kurrichane Thrush *Turdus libonyana*

21–23cm Sexes similar. A woodland thrush with slate grey-brown head and upperparts, whitish belly and brown-orange flanks. Bright orange bill and white throat with distinct black malar stripes are diagnostic. (See African Thrush.) Eye is brown with narrow orange eye-ring. Juv. breast and flanks are densely spotted over yellowish wash. Upperparts have scalloped appearance. **Status:** Common widespread resident, singly or in pairs. **Habitat:** Any woodland type, particularly miombo; also gardens. **Voice:** Distinctive loud, high-pitched whistle.

Bearded Scrub Robin
Cercotrichas quadrivirgata

16–17cm Sexes similar. A warmly-coloured robin with distinct black-and-white head pattern with white eyebrow and black moustachial stripe. Upperparts and ear coverts are brown. Breast, flanks and rump are rufous, wing spots clear white. Juv. has mottled upperparts and breast. **Status:** Fairly common resident in Lower Zambezi, South Luangwa and southern edge of Kafue Flats. **Habitat:** Dense understorey of dry riparian forest and thickets in broad-leaved woodland. **Voice:** Variety of musical whistles.

Miombo Scrub Robin *Cercotrichas barbata*

17cm Sexes similar. Similar to Bearded Scrub Robin with more extensive rufous underparts, rich rufous ear coverts and greyer back. (Bearded Scrub Robin has brown ear coverts.) Juv. is scaled black above and buff below. **Status:** Widespread and locally common in pairs. Geographically separated from Bearded Scrub Robin. **Habitat:** Miombo woodland, particularly understorey of mature woodland with scattered thickets, and *Cryptosepalum* forest in the west. **Voice:** Calls from deep within dense vegetation. Loud, rapid, varied series of high-pitched whistles.

White-browed Scrub Robin
Cercotrichas leucophrys

14–16cm Sexes similar. A common scrub robin with olive-brown upperparts, rufous rump and uppertail coverts, and blackish wings with diagnostic double white wingbar. Head is grey-brown with clear white supercilium. Underparts are white with dark brown streaking on breast. Juv. has spotted buff upperparts and mottled breast. **Status:** Common widespread resident throughout. **Habitat:** Most woodland types but avoids dense woodland. **Voice:** Wide range of musical whistles that are repeated for some time.

Grey Tit-Flycatcher   *Myioparus plumbeus*

14cm Sexes similar. A slender, apalis-like bird with slate-grey upperparts, pale grey breast and white belly. Black tail with white outer tail feathers is regularly fanned and flirted in diagnostic movement. (No white eye-ring or loral stripe like similar Ashy Flycatcher.) Juv. has speckled brown upperparts and underparts. **Status:** Widespread resident singly or in pairs; will join bird parties. **Habitat:** Miombo and other woodland, thickets and edges of riparian forest. Often in transition zones. **Voice:** Soft but far-reaching, mournful whistle.

Southern Black Flycatcher
Melaenornis pammelaina

19–22cm Sexes similar. A small all-black flycatcher with dark brown eye and diagnostic tail, either square-ended or with very slight fork. (Similar larger Fork-tailed Drongo has deep red eye and deeply forked tail.) Female is a deeper brownish-black. Juv. has brown upper- and underparts with grey mottling. **Status:** Common widespread resident in pairs with local movements, often together with Fork-tailed Drongo. Joins mixed bird parties. **Habitat:** Various open woodland types throughout Zambia. **Voice:** Series of soft, high-pitched whistles or warbles.

Pale Flycatcher   *Melaenornis pallidus*

15–17cm Sexes similar. A somewhat uniformly-coloured flycatcher, with grey-brown upperparts and light grey underparts. Often flicks wings and tail. Birds in south and west are slightly larger, paler and greyer. Juv. has mottled brown and grey plumage. **Status:** Common throughout, apart from Lower Zambezi and Luangwa Valley; usually in pairs. Occasionally joins mixed flocks. **Habitat:** Open miombo and other woodland types, wooded grassland. Seldom in mopane or *Acacia*. **Voice:** Series of high-pitched warbles and rasping notes.

Spotted Flycatcher   *Muscicapa striata*

14cm Sexes similar. A small flycatcher with grey-brown upperparts and whitish underparts. Crown is streaked brown, and breast and flanks are also lightly streaked. Juv. is more heavily streaked. **Status:** Common Palaearctic migrant occurring October to April, usually singly. **Habitat:** Any open woodland type, wooded grassland, edges of thickets, gardens and plantations where suitable raised hunting perches are available. **Voice:** Harsh single or double chirp.

Ashy Flycatcher   *Muscicapa caerulescens*

13–15cm Sexes similar. An ashy-grey flycatcher with distinctive white eye-ring. Lores are black with white stripe above. Underparts are pale with faint grey tinge on breast and flanks; shortish grey tail is square-ended. Juv. has heavily spotted upperparts and mottled underparts. **Status:** Common widespread resident, usually in pairs. Scarce in extreme west. Darts from perch and returns – feeding aerially with beak snapping loudly. Often in mixed bird parties. **Habitat:** Wide variety of forest and well-wooded habitats including miombo. **Voice:** High-pitched four-syllable song.

Lee Gutteridge

Swamp Flycatcher   *Muscicapa aquatica*

13–14cm Sexes similar. A small aquatic flycatcher with dark brown upperparts, bill, lores and legs. White throat and belly are separated by a broad buffy-brown breast band. Juv. has buff spots on upperparts and light streaking on breast. **Status:** Locally common resident always by permanent water; at swamps in the north as well as Kafue Flats. **Habitat:** Favours papyrus swamps but also tall patches of *Aeschynomene elaphroxylon*. **Voice:** High-pitched squeaky song.

Jean van der Meulen / Pixabay

African Dusky Flycatcher
Muscicapa adusta

12–13cm Sexes similar. A small, dumpy flycatcher with grey-brown upperparts and dusky underparts with faint smudges on breast. Very faint streaking on crown. Juv. has buff spots on upperparts and brown spots on white underparts. **Status:** Locally common. Seasonal altitudinal movements of non-br. birds to low valleys in south and east from December to July. **Habitat:** Edges of evergreen and riparian forests, well-developed miombo woodland and edges of plantations. **Voice:** Very high-pitched chittering.

Nik Borrow

Böhm's Flycatcher   *Muscicapa boehmi*

12–13cm Sexes similar. A small and compact flycatcher with brown upperparts and buffy edge to feathers. Underparts are white with diagnostic well-defined triangular black marks on breast and flanks. Juv. is dark brown above with dark spots on head; underparts are white with dark crescents on breast. **Status:** Uncommon near-endemic, usually in pairs or mixed bird parties. **Habitat:** Well-developed miombo woodland; absent from the miombo woodlands in Luangwa Valley and the south. **Voice:** Various soft, warbling and zitting notes.

White-browed Robin-Chat
Cossypha heuglini

19–20cm Sexes similar. A large robin-chat with black crown, clear white supercilium, black cheeks, grey mantle and back, and all-rufous underparts. Juv. is mottled, lacks eye-stripe. **Status:** Common widespread resident, usually in pairs. **Habitat:** Variety of dense habitats, including woodland thickets, forest edges and suburbia. **Voice:** Varied series of loud, melodious whistles that rise and fall in pitch. A common garden songster in the early mornings and late evenings.

Red-capped Robin-Chat
Cossypha natalensis

16–17cm Sexes similar. A robin-chat with rufous face and underparts, and slate-grey wings and back. Crown is light olive-brown, rump rufous-brown. Juv. upperparts with buff spots, underparts mottled black. **Status:** Intra-African br. migrant September to March. Resident year-round in Mwinilunga. **Habitat:** Ground-stratum in evergreen forest including *Cryptosepalum*, riparian thickets. **Voice:** Mixed series of melodious and mournful sounds with superb mimicry, including repetitive 'see-saw' notes.

Albert Froneman

White-starred Robin   *Pogonocichla stellata*

15–16cm Sexes similar. A small forest robin with slate-grey head and throat, bright yellow underparts and two white spots or 'stars' on grey face (usually concealed unless displaying). Tail is yellow with black centre. Juv. is blackish-brown above with yellow speckles, pale yellow below with dark brown scaling. **Status:** Locally common resident on Nyika Plateau, north to Mafinga Mountains. Males resident, females and juveniles altitudinal migrants after breeding. **Habitat:** Restricted to montane forests. **Voice:** Two- to three-note 'too-twee' whistle.

Roy Glasspool

Bocage's Akalat   *Sheppardia bocage*

13cm Sexes similar. A small robin with grey upperparts and slight olive wash on crown. Underparts orange-rufous with whitish belly. Wings and tail are dull brown. Juv. is dark above with rufous spots, heavily mottled rufous-buff and black below. **Status:** Uncommon secretive resident in most of northwest and Mafinga Mountains in the northeast. Absent from extreme northwest. **Habitat:** Moist evergreen forest; riverine and montane forest. **Voice:** High-pitched musical song.

Collared Palm Thrush   *Cichladusa arquata*

17–18cm Sexes similar. A strongly marked palm thrush with rufous wings and tail, buffy-cream throat and upper breast, with a black 'necklace' border running to base of the bill, and creamy eyes. Cap is rufous, face, neck and sides of breast grey, belly and flanks buffy. Juv. throat is buffier, with little or no black 'necklace'. **Status:** Common localised resident, with an isolated population in the extreme west. **Habitat:** Thickets with palms (*Borassus, Hyphaene* and *Raphia*). **Voice:** Melodious mix of whistles and growls.

Nik Borrow; Inset: Piet Zwanniken

Miombo Rock Thrush   *Monticola angolensis*

16–18cm A long-legged rock thrush. Male has blue-grey head and upperparts with variable black streaking or spotting. Underparts are dull orange with buffy centre to belly and undertail coverts. Female has mottled buff-and-black upperparts, orange tail and sides of breast, and distinctive black malar stripe. Juv. is spotted buff, white and black above, whitish below with orange wash on mottled breast. **Status:** Common localised resident, usually in pairs. **Habitat:** Miombo woodlands on central plateau; rocky miombo on Luangwa Valley and Lower Zambezi escarpments. **Voice:** Melodious whistle.

African Stonechat *Saxicola torquatus*

13–14cm Male has diagnostic combination of black head and back, chestnut breast and white patch on neck. Female is duller with buff-coloured back and head, streaked dark brown. Both sexes show white patches in wing and a white rump. Juv. is buff-coloured, heavily speckled on upperparts, with streaked breast and flanks. **Status:** Locally common resident; occasionally in Luangwa Valley and Lower Zambezi. **Habitat:** Grassland, edges of swamps and dambos, montane grassland with small bushes and bracken–briar. **Voice:** Quiet warble; alarm a sharp 'chit'.

Mocking Cliff Chat
Thamnolaea cinnamomeiventris

19–21cm A brightly-coloured, rock-loving chat. Glossy black male has a white shoulder patch, chestnut rump, vent and belly, and thin white line across upper belly. Female is duller, dark grey above with dark rufous underparts and no white shoulder patch. Juv. is duller overall. **Status:** Locally common resident in pairs or family groups. **Habitat:** Rocky areas such as well-wooded cliff faces, gorges and koppies; also areas of human habitation in vicinity of large boulders. **Voice:** Musical whistles and trills.

Sooty Chat *Myrmecocichla nigra*

16–18cm A medium-sized chat. Male is glossy black with white shoulder patch. Female is dark chocolate brown with no shoulder patch. (Similar juv. Arnott's Chat has black head, more white in wings, longer tail and occupies different habitat.) **Status:** Locally common resident. **Habitat:** Dry dambos and plains on the central plateau. Favours short-grass areas with termitaria, aardvark holes, farmland, culverts, old mud buildings and recently burnt ground. **Voice:** Song a mixture of musical whistles and occasional growling notes.

Leanne Mackay

Roy Glasspool; Inset: Stephanie McDougal

♀   ♂

Arnott's Chat   *Myrmecocichla arnotti*

16–18cm A black-and-white chat. Male is black with white crown and large white shoulder patch. Female has a black crown and white throat. Juv. male is black with no white feathers on crown, shoulder patches are white; second season shows a few white markings, especially on supercilium. Juv. female has white throat and shoulders. **Status:** Common widespread resident in pairs and family groups. **Habitat:** Dry miombo and primary mopane woodland with open understorey. Some adapted to human habitation. **Voice:** Soft, high-pitched squeaky notes.

Capped Wheatear   *Oenanthe pileata*

16–18cm Sexes similar. A striking wheatear with broad black breast band separating white throat from white underparts. Black on cap and face runs down sides of neck to breast band; forehead band and supercilium are white. Juv. is brown above with buff spots, off-white below, and more mottled breast. **Status:** Intra-African br. migrant mid-May to December; some year-round. **Habitat:** Short grassland in dry floodplains and dambos, mostly overgrazed or recently burnt areas, airfields and montane parts. **Voice:** Series of short, jumbled whistles, trills and harsh notes.

Familiar Chat   *Oenanthe familiaris*

14–15cm Sexes similar. A pale chat with grey-brown upperparts, head and neck, and reddish-brown cheeks. Underparts are grey; rump and tail are rufous-orange. Dark brown inner tail feathers and tip of tail form a diagnostic 'T' shape. The Zambian race *O. f. falkensteini* does not wing-flick. **Status:** Common localised resident. **Habitat:** Rocky areas and escarpments in upper-eastern parts of Kafue, Mwinilunga and Lower Zambezi escarpment. Also around Victoria Falls. Often found around human habitation. **Voice:** Harsh 'chuk' alarm call. Song a soft, whistled chattering.

Anchieta's Sunbird   *Anthreptes anchietae*

10–12cm Sexes similar. A bright sunbird with brown upperparts and iridescent blue crown, throat and upper breast. Breast and belly are red and yellow, undertail coverts brown. Female is duller. Juv. is similar to female with olive-yellow underparts. **Status:** Locally common resident. **Habitat:** Mature miombo woodlands and dambo ecotone. Mwinilunga district in northwest; plateau in north and northeast. **Voice:** Various high-pitched, soft chirps and whistles.

Dan Danckwerts

Western Violet-backed Sunbird
Anthreptes longuemarei

13–14cm Br. male has violet head and upperparts and white underparts. Female has brown head and back, white supercilium and throat, and pale yellow belly. The non-br. male is mottled with brown feathers in-between violet upperparts. Juv. is similar to female, with yellow breast and belly. **Status:** Fairly common resident throughout plateau; absent from major river valleys. **Habitat:** Miombo woodlands and edges of riparian forest. **Voice:** Jumble of high-pitched warbles and chirps.

Piet Zwanniken   ♂

Collared Sunbird   *Hedydipna collaris*

9–10cm Tiny with diagnostic short, slightly curved bill. Both sexes have metallic-green upperparts and bright yellow underparts. Male throat is metallic green with a narrow purple breast band and yellow pectoral tufts. Female entirely yellow below. (Male Variable Sunbird is larger with longer, more curved bill, larger purple breast band and orange pectoral tufts. Female Variable Sunbird lacks metallic-green upperparts.) Juv. resembles female. **Status:** Common widespread resident; avoids *Baikiaea* woodland in west. **Habitat:** Canopy, edges of evergreen and riparian forest. **Voice:** High-pitched 'chewy' call.

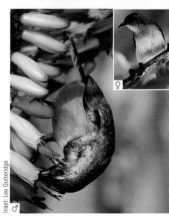

Inset: Lee Gutteridge   ♂

Stephanie McDougall

Olive Sunbird   *Cyanomitra olivacea*

12–15cm Sexes similar. A large olive-green sunbird with long, decurved bill. Upperparts are darker than underparts. Pectoral tufts are yellow or orange. Juv. is yellower on throat and breast. **Status:** Common forest resident in north down to the Nyika and Luangwa Valley escarpment. Westwards to North Western Province. Isolated population from Lusaka to the Zambezi escarpment only where there is suitable riparian vegetation. **Habitat:** Moist forest or thickets including *Cryptosephalum*. **Voice:** Melodious whistles with chitting notes in-between.

Albert Froneman/Images of Africa

Albert Froneman/Images of Africa

Amethyst Sunbird   *Chalcomitra amethystina*

13–15cm Male plumage appears all-black; forehead is metallic green, throat and shoulder patches are reddish-purple. Female is grey-brown above with pale malar stripe. Underparts are pale yellow-grey, chin and throat streaked. Juv. is yellowish below with black throat; upper breast is densely mottled black and yellow. **Status:** Common widespread resident. **Habitat:** Well-developed woodlands such as miombo, *Baikiaea* and *Cryptosepalum*, and edges of riparian forest; also gardens. **Voice:** High-pitched, loud chips and twitters.

Grant Reed

Scarlet-chested Sunbird
Chalcomitra senegalensis

13–15cm Male is a distinctive, deep black, with long, curved bill and bright scarlet breast. Forehead and throat are iridescent green; shoulder patch iridescent violet. Female is similar to Amethyst Sunbird but lacks supercilium, and mottling on the breast is heavier. Obvious white alula. Juv. is like female but chin is blacker, with traces of scarlet and green on throat of juv. male. **Status:** Very common resident. **Habitat:** Variety of open woodland types, especially miombo; also edges of riparian forest, thickets and gardens. **Voice:** Repetitive, fairly harsh chipping call.

Eastern Miombo Sunbird
Cinnyris manoensis

15–16cm Male's head, throat and mantle are glossy green; breast band is red with narrow blue band above. Underparts and rump are olive-grey, uppertail coverts blue. Female is grey-brown above, with buffy grey on throat and breast, and yellowish wash on belly. Juv. is similar to female with stronger yellow wash below. **Status:** Common localised resident. **Habitat:** Miombo woodland, preferring rocky areas with sparser vegetation. **Voice:** High-pitched warble, usually preceded by one or two 'chip' notes.

Western Miombo Sunbird
Cinnyris gertrudis

11–12cm Compact sunbird. Head, throat, mantle and uppertail are glossy green. Bright red breast band has narrow blue band above. Long yellow pectoral tufts. Uppertail coverts grey-green. Underparts and rump olive-grey. Female has grey-yellow upperparts, blackish wash on head and wings, and yellowish underparts. Juv. similar to female, more yellow below. **Status:** Common localised resident. **Habitat:** Miombo woodland; common in rocky areas. **Voice:** High-pitched warble ends with descending 1.5-second trill.

Stephanie McDougall

Shelley's Sunbird
Cinnyris shelleyi

9–13cm The male has striking iridescent green upperparts, a broad scarlet breast band, and black wings and tail. Belly is black, uppertail coverts green. (See Eastern Miombo Sunbird.) Female is plain, speckled on throat and upper breast. (No speckling in female Eastern Miombo Sunbird.) Juv. throat and upper breast are black with dark markings on breast and flanks. **Status:** Common on eastern plateau. Uncommon in Luangwa Valley and Lower Zambezi. **Habitat:** Dry escarpment miombo woodland; occasionally *in Baikiaea* forest. **Voice:** A fast series of high-pitched warbles.

Nik Borrow

Grant Reed

Purple-banded Sunbird   *Cinnyris bifasciatus*

9–11cm Small sunbird with less decurved bill. Br. male has iridescent green upperparts, head, throat and upper breast, with a narrow purple breast band. Underparts are black. Female is grey-white below with indistinct streaking. Juv. is like female but with dark throat. **Status:** Locally common resident in parts of northern and northwest Zambia; irregular in other areas. **Habitat:** Edge of riparian and other evergreen forest, dense termitaria thickets, and gardens. **Voice:** Short, high-pitched phrases or harsher trills.

White-bellied Sunbird   *Cinnyris talatala*

10–12cm Small sunbird. Male has metallic-green upperparts including face and neck. Bright yellow pectoral tufts. Breast band is violet with narrow black band below. Belly is white, sometimes pale yellow. Tail is short. Female is olive-brown above, off-white below with faint streaks on breast. Juv. similar to female with blackish throat in juv. male. **Status:** Common widespread resident. **Habitat:** Dry woodlands of southern Zambia, particularly mopane, *Baikiaea* and *Acacia*. A regular garden visitor. **Voice:** High-pitched trill; two- or three-note 'cheep' or 'chew'.

Variable Sunbird   *Cinnyris venustus*

10–11cm Male has metallic-green upperparts, black tail and wings, a broad purple breast band and long curved bill. (See Collared Sunbird.) Underparts are deep yellow, pectoral tufts orange or yellow. Female upperparts are grey-brown, underparts buffy-yellow with no streaking, tail black. Juv. male has black speckled throat. Juv. female is similar to adult female. **Status:** Common resident throughout, apart from extreme south. **Habitat:** Rank growth along streams, edges of riparian forest and moist thickets. **Voice:** Repetitive, high-pitched warbles or trills; call is one to four squeaky notes.

Copper Sunbird
Cinnyris cupreus

12–13cm Br. male has unmistakable coppery sheen with black belly, wings and short tail. No pectoral tufts. Non-br. male like female, with coppery gloss on wing coverts, dark blotches on yellow underparts. Female is dull olive-grey above, pale yellow below. Juv. female like adult; juv. male like non-br. male. **Status:** Locally common resident on plateau; local movement into valleys. **Habitat:** Woodland/floodplain ecotone, edges of riparian forest and open *Cryptosepalum*–miombo woodland. **Voice:** Mix of high-pitched 'chit' notes, metallic warbles and squeaky notes.

Nik Borrow

♂ ♀

Northern Grey-headed Sparrow
Passer griseus

15–16cm Sexes similar. A plain sparrow with grey head, nape and underparts. Wings and tail dark brown. (Slightly larger than similar Southern Grey-headed Sparrow.) Large all-black bill, white throat; sometimes has a small white wing-patch. Juv. lacks white wing patch; has horn-coloured bill. **Status:** Fairly common resident, range expanding across Zambia from the northeast. Mainly absent from extreme west. **Habitat:** Mainly around human settlements, though less common than House Sparrow. **Voice:** Repeated 'cheerp'.

Lee Gutteridge

Southern Grey-headed Sparrow
Passer diffusus

14–15cm Sexes similar. A plain sparrow with pale grey head and nape, pale rufous-brown back, and chestnut rump and wings with clear white wingbar. (See Northern Grey-headed Sparrow.) Underparts are pale grey, throat whitish to pale grey. Bill is dark horn-brown, only becoming black in breeding season. Juv. is duller. **Status:** Common resident in the south and west. In pairs during breeding, sometimes forming large post-br. flocks. **Habitat:** Open woodland types including mopane and mixed *Acacia*–*Combretum* woodland. **Voice:** A bubbling 'chirrup'.

Yellow-throated Petronia
Gymnoris superciliaris

15–16cm Sexes similar. A sparrow with greyish-brown, dusky-streaked upperparts, plain brown crown, and prominent, broad, straight, whitish-buff eyebrow. Two pale narrow wingbars; yellow throat-spot is seldom seen. Bill is pointed. Juv. is similar to adult but lacks yellow throat. Birds on eastern plateau are paler overall and browner, while extreme northwest birds appear darker. **Status:** Locally common resident. In pairs, often in mixed bird parties. **Habitat:** Broad-leaved woodland throughout. **Voice:** Typical two- to four-note 'trit-trit' call.

♀

♂

Red-billed Buffalo Weaver
Bubalornis niger

21–24cm A large, heavy-billed weaver. Male is blackish-brown with orange-red bill; shows variable white flecks on shoulder, neck, flanks and edges of primary feathers. Female upperparts are dark brown, underparts mottled brown and white. Bill varies from pale red to horn-coloured. Juv. is similar to female, but underparts spotted and barred with white. **Status:** Localised resident in Luangwa Valley and Lower Zambezi, also above Victoria Falls up to Kafue. **Habitat:** Mopane and *Acacia* woodland. **Voice:** Series of chattering notes.

White-browed Sparrow-Weaver
Plocepasser mahali

16–18cm Sexes similar. A large, noisy, boldly marked weaver with broad white eye-stripe and two prominent white wingbars. Mantle and back are reddish-brown, underparts mostly white with brown breast spots. Male has black bill, female pale brown. Juv. is drabber with pale bill. **Status:** Common localised cooperative breeding resident in Luangwa Valley and Lower Zambezi, southern Kafue Flats and parts of southern plateau. **Habitat:** Favours mopane woodland, also tall marula and *Acacia* woodland. **Voice:** Repetitive, prolonged chattering and shrill notes.

Spectacled Weaver   *Ploceus ocularis*

14–16cm Sexes similar. A striking weaver with olive-green upperparts and bright yellow underparts. Bill is black, long and pointed. Diagnostic narrow black mask from the base of bill through the eye. Eye is pale yellow. Male has black throat. Juv. is duller with olive eye-stripe and brown bill. **Status:** Widespread localised resident. Scarce in southwest. Mostly in pairs and bird parties. **Habitat:** Riparian forest margins and thickets, gardens, rank dense reedbeds and grasses. **Voice:** Distinctive descending series of whistled 'tee-tee-tee' notes.

Inset: Roy Glasspool

Holub's Golden Weaver   *Ploceus xanthops*

16–18cm Sexes similar. A large golden-yellow weaver with greenish wash to upperparts, pale yellow eye and large, heavy black bill. Male has orange wash on throat and upper breast. Female is duller with no orange wash on throat. Juv. is buffy yellow below, with brown eye and bill. **Status:** Widespread locally common resident in small sedentary colonies. **Habitat:** Edges of woodland, forest, thickets and reedbeds, all usually near water. Also gardens and cultivated lands. **Voice:** Contact or alarm call is harsh 'tzit'.

Lee Gutteridge

Lesser Masked Weaver
Ploceus intermedius

13–14cm A small masked weaver with diagnostic white or pale yellow eye and grey legs. Black mask extends from top of crown to form a rounded bib in br. male. Upperparts are greenish-yellow, underparts yellow. Non-br. male loses black mask. Female and non-br. male have yellow-olive upperparts with light streaking and a white belly, but br. female is all yellow. Juv. has brown eye and legs. **Status:** Common resident, distribution patchy. Breeds colonially. **Habitat:** Dry woodlands, especially *Acacia*, seldom far from water. **Voice:** Loud, swizzling song.

Southern Masked Weaver   *Ploceus velatus*

13–14cm Br. male is bright yellow with black face extending from forehead (just above bill) to a pointed bib. Crown is bright yellow. Eye is red, bill is black, legs flesh-coloured. Female and non-br. male are dull, with streaky olive-brown upperparts, and buffy-white belly. Eye is brown, red in br. females; bill horn-coloured. Juv. is similar to non-br. female. **Status:** Common colonial resident in southern half of Zambia. **Habitat:** Dry, open woodland, particularly *Acacia*. Also old cultivation and rural gardens. **Voice:** Song is a series of high-pitched swizzling notes.

Village Weaver   *Ploceus cucullatus*

15–17cm A masked weaver with mottled yellow-and-black upperparts and red eye. Br. male has black head and nape and yellow underparts. Non-br. male and female have dull olive head, mottled grey-yellow back and grey-white underparts. Eye is red-brown. Juv. is like female with pale brown bill and dark brown eye. **Status:** Widespread common resident. Breeds colonially near water, wandering into woodland to forage. **Habitat:** Various woodland types, reedbeds and palms near water. Avoids high-lying areas. **Voice:** Song an extended series of harsh swizzling notes.

Dark-backed Weaver   *Ploceus bicolor*

14–16cm Sexes similar. A large weaver with upperparts including head, mantle and back blackish-brown, and underparts bright yellow. Eye is dark red, bill black or blue-grey, and legs flesh-coloured. Juv. is similar to adult but duller. **Status:** This common forest weaver is a localised resident in northern Zambia. Also an isolated race around Siavonga near Lake Kariba. Occurs in bird parties. **Habitat:** Evergreen wet forests in northern Zambia, dry, deciduous thickets in Middle Zambezi. **Voice:** High-pitched, chittering contact call.

Lee Gutteridge

Bar-winged Weaver   *Ploceus angolensis*

13cm Sexes similar. Weaver with slender bill, dark brown head, brown back with cream mantle and yellow rump; wings have two narrow white wingbars. Underparts white, yellow wash on belly. Juv. has olive-grey crown with narrow white eye-stripe. **Status:** Uncommon localised resident, mixes in bird parties. **Habitat:** Well-developed miombo and lichen-covered *Cryptosephalum* woodland on northern plateau. Dependent on Old Man's Beard (*Usnea barbata*) and lichens. **Voice:** Contact call a chirp or musical whistle; flight call a descending trill.

Dan Danckwerts

Red-headed Weaver   *Anaplectes rubriceps*

12–15cm A grey-backed weaver. Br. male has scarlet head and breast, and grey upperparts with bright yellow edges to flight feathers and greater coverts. Underparts are white and bill orange-red in all plumages. Female and non-br. male have orange-yellow to yellow head and breast. Juv. is similar to non-br. adults but duller. **Status:** Common widespread resident in small family groups, often mixes in bird parties. **Habitat:** Open broad-leafed woodland. **Voice:** Squeaky, chattering song.

Albert Froneman/Images of Africa

♂

Red-billed Quelea   *Quelea quelea*

11–12cm A compact weaver. Br. male has black or white face mask; head colour varies from red to straw-brown to creamy white. Male has red bill, female yellow. Non-br. male and female have mottled greyish-brown upperparts, off-white eye-stripe, greyish-white underparts and red bill. Juv. is similar to non-br. adults with horn-coloured bill. **Status:** Highly gregarious in massive nomadic flocks in medium- to low-lying areas. Widespread but sparse in the well-wooded, high-rainfall habitats. **Habitat:** Prefers semi-arid areas. **Voice:** A loud, chattering chorus.

Inset: Lee Gutteridge

br. ♀

br. ♂

Black-winged Red Bishop
Euplectes hordeaceus

12cm Br. male crown is totally red, wing feathers and tail black. Non-br. male retains black wings and tail. Female and non-br. male have mottled greyish-brown upperparts, pale buff underparts with brown streaks on throat and upper breast, and dull yellow-white supercilium. Juv. is similar to female and non-br. male. **Status:** Patchy resident on most of plateau; absent from west and south. Prefers high rainfall areas. **Habitat:** Tall rank stream vegetation, dambos, moist areas in miombo. **Voice:** Buzzy, chattering series of notes.

Southern Red Bishop   *Euplectes orix*

13–14cm A large red bishop. Br. male has black forecrown, red crown, red back and rump, with brown wings and tail. Underparts are black, undertail coverts red. Female and non-br. male have mottled grey-brown upperparts, and pale buff underparts with brown streaks on throat and upper breast. Juv. is similar but underparts darker. **Status:** Common localised resident; absent from large parts of wetter regions in the north. **Habitat:** Open marshy areas with tall grass or reeds. **Voice:** Metallic swizzling.

Yellow Bishop   *Euplectes capensis*

17cm Br. male is all-black with yellow shoulders and yellow rump. Upper mandible is black, lower mandible white. Female and non-br. male have mottled greyish-brown upperparts, and buff underparts with heavy streaking on throat and breast. Non-br. male retains yellow rump and scapulars. Female has dull mustard-yellow shoulder patch. Juv. is like female, but no shoulder patch. **Status:** Common on central plateau and northwest Zambia. **Habitat:** Rank vegetation with scattered trees and bushes including the edges of woodland. **Voice:** Metallic chipping swizzling song.

Fan-tailed Widowbird *Euplectes axillaris*

15–17cm A shorter-tailed widowbird. Br. male is black with broad, fan-shaped tail. Bill is pale blue-grey; shoulder is orange-yellow, red in southern Zambia. Non-br. male is heavily streaked above with orange-yellow scapulars, black primaries, buff throat and breast, and russet underwing coverts. Supercilium is distinct. Female is like non-br. male with brown primaries; orange-yellow shoulder is indistinct, bill horn-coloured. Juv. like female. **Status:** Common resident in wet regions in west and north; absent from east. **Habitat:** Tall, swampy grassland. **Voice:** Sizzling call.

Yellow-mantled Widowbird
Euplectes macroura

13–14cm (br. male 19–20cm) Br. male is black with yellow mantle and shoulders, and long, black, rounded tail. Non-br. male has black primaries, yellow scapulars, short brown tail. Female and non-br. male are light brown above, with dark central feather streaks and pale buff eyebrow. Underparts are pale buff with some light streaking on breast. Juv. has yellow wash on underparts. **Status:** Locally common resident. **Habitat:** Dambos, other moist short grasslands with trees. **Voice:** High-pitched twittering, buzzy notes.

non-br. ♀

non-br. ♂

Leanne Mackay

♂

Marsh Widowbird *Euplectes hartlaubi*

15–18cm (br. male 36cm) Br. male is all-black with long tail, yellow scapulars with buff border, and a pale grey-blue bill. Non-br. male has black primaries and retains yellow shoulder patch; upperparts are dark brown with buffy margins to the feathers, a short brown tail and tawny-white underparts. Female and juv. have brown primaries, no shoulder patch, buff underparts and pale brown bill. **Status:** Common localised resident in north and northwest. Mixes with other widowbirds. **Habitat:** Large moist dambos with scattered trees. **Voice:** High-pitched trilling.

♀

Roy Glasspool x2

♂

White-winged Widowbird
Euplectes albonotatus

14cm Br. male is black with medium-length, fan-shaped tail. Scapulars are yellow with white wing-patch. Bill is blue-grey. Non-br. male has black wings with white margins, and yellow scapulars. Both sexes (non-br.) have mottled grey-brown upperparts and buffy yellow underparts with no breast streaking. Bill is blue in male, brown in female. Juv. resembles female. **Status:** Locally common resident in drier south-central, eastern half and far northern parts. **Habitat:** *Acacia* and other dry, open woodland. **Voice:** Chipping, buzzy notes.

Red-collared Widowbird   *Euplectes ardens*

12–13cm (br. male 30cm) Br. male all-black with red crescent-shaped collar and long, floppy tail. Bill and legs black. Non-br. male and female streaky brown above with big yellowish supercilium, buff breast and paler unstreaked belly; bill brown. Non-br. male keeps black primaries; back and tail feathers black with buffy edges. Juv. similar to female, darker buff below. **Status:** Common resident apart from Lower Luangwa and Zambezi valleys and far west; scarce on southern plateau. **Habitat:** Wet and dry rank grass, dambos. **Voice:** Soft, high-pitched rapid trill.

Orange-winged Pytilia   *Pytilia afra*

11–13cm Darker than the Green-winged Pytilia. Male has red forehead, throat and ear coverts. Orange wing panel is barred olive and white below. Both sexes have red rump, eye and bill. Female has all-grey head. Juv. is browner above, has dark brown eye. **Status:** Common localised resident, easily overlooked. Scarce in Western Province. Congregates in small, nomadic, post-br. flocks. Brood host to Broad-tailed Paradise Whydah. **Habitat:** Any herbaceous understorey in most woodland, prefers miombo and *Baikiaea*, seldom in *Acacia*. **Voice:** Short buzzy call or soft contact whistle.

Green-winged Pytilia   *Pytilia melba*

12–14cm Male has bright red forehead, chin and throat; rest of head including ear coverts is grey. (See Orange-winged Pytilia.) Wings are olive-green, back yellowish-green. Underparts are boldly barred black and white. Female has all-grey head and throat. Juv. is similar to female with less obvious barring below. **Status:** Locally common resident in lower rainfall areas. Brood host to Long-tailed Paradise Whydah. **Habitat:** Drier woodland thickets and understorey, especially *Acacia* in lower rainfall areas. **Voice:** Long trill or a buzzy series of notes.

♀   ♂

Cut-throat Finch   *Amadina fasciata*

11–12cm A strongly patterned finch. Male is unmistakable with broad red throat-band. Both sexes are heavily barred on head, neck and throat. Bill is light blue-grey. Female is duller with no throat patch. Juv. is similar to female, with male showing narrow red throat stripe. **Status:** Locally common resident mainly in south, with some local movement, particularly in the dry months. An isolated population in South Luangwa valley is subject to local movements. **Habitat:** Dry open woodland, particularly *Acacia* and mopane. **Voice:** High-pitched, quiet 'chip' notes.

♀

♂

Red-throated Twinspot
Hypargos niveoguttatus

12–13cm Male has grey crown and face, and crimson-red throat and upper breast. Round white spots on black lower breast and belly; back and wings brown, rump dark red. Female has grey face, buffy-orange-washed breast, and flanks with white spots. Juv. has brown crown and grey underparts with no white spotting. **Status:** Common resident in low-lying parts of north, Luangwa and Zambezi valleys, and centre of the country. **Habitat:** Dense undergrowth in thickets and forest edges. **Voice:** High-pitched series of tinny, melodious notes.

Roddy Smith   ♂

Roddy Smith   ♀

Marc Cronje

Marc Cronje

Brown Firefinch *Lagonosticta nitidula*

9–10cm A lacklustre firefinch with grey-brown upperparts, including the rump (red in all other firefinch species). Male has a red face, throat and upper breast, with white spots on sides of breast; bill is red. Female is duller with faint pink wash on face and throat. Juv. is all-brown with dark brown bill. **Status:** Locally common resident in pairs or family groups. Absent from south-central and eastern regions. **Habitat:** Edges of evergreen and riparian forests, and thickets. **Voice:** Various trills and whistles while singing; alarm or contact rattles interspersed with trills.

Red-billed Firefinch *Lagonosticta senegala*

9–10cm A red-billed finch with brown upperparts and yellow eye-ring. Male has red head, underparts and rump, with white spots on sides of breast. Female has red lores, grey-brown head and upperparts; underparts with light pink wash, and grey lower breast and belly. Juv. is similar to female but with black bill, no eye-ring, and lacks white spots on sides of breast. **Status:** Locally common resident. **Habitat:** Dry, open woodland, *Acacia*, thickets, secondary growth around human habitation and suburbia. **Voice:** A mixture of bubbling trills and whistles.

Marc Cronje

Marc Cronje

African Firefinch *Lagonosticta rubricata*

10–11cm A richly coloured finch with grey-brown back and wings with no red wash. Rump is red, bill dark blue-black. Male has grey crown, and deep red face and underparts. Black undertail coverts are diagnostic. Female is duller with pinkish-brown underparts. Juv. has brown underparts; only rump is red. **Status:** Common localised resident in the wetter two-thirds of country, in pairs and family groups. **Habitat:** Drier rank vegetation in thickets, edge of riverine and evergreen forest. Also montane bracken–briar. **Voice:** Variety of melodious whistles and trills; rattling alarm or contact call.

Jameson's Firefinch
Lagonosticta rhodopareia

10–11cm Firefinch with pink face, nape and back; crown has a pink wash. Flight feathers are brown, rump red, bill dark blue-grey. Female is paler with greyish-pink head and dull pink underparts. Juv. is duller and browner than female. **Status:** Locally common resident in pairs or family groups, often with other seedeaters. **Habitat:** Dry habitats such as semi-arid bush, tall grasses, thickets, edges of riparian forest in drier areas, weeds and scrub. **Voice:** Mixture of high-pitched trills and whistles. Soft, purring alarm call.

Blue Waxbill
Uraeginthus angolensis

12–13cm Sexes similar. A striking blue finch with brown upperparts, crown and wings. Uppertail coverts and tail are distinctive blue; face, throat, breast and flanks also blue; belly and vent buffy white. Bill is pale-grey. Female has paler blue face, throat and upper breast. Juv. is like female but duller. **Status:** Common resident in drier two-thirds of country. Occurs in pairs and family groups, often with other seedeaters. **Habitat:** Thickets, scrubland, woodland edges, cultivation, gardens. **Voice:** Song is high-pitched tinny notes; contact call a soft, buzzy trill.

Fawn-breasted Waxbill
Estrilda paludicola

9–10cm Sexes similar. A plain waxbill with dark grey head and lighter cheek and lores. Back and wings are brown. Rump is bright red, tail black, and bill red. Underparts are buff with yellow wash on centre of belly. Vent has red tips to feathers. Female is duller with brown crown. Juv. has darker upperparts with whiter underparts and black bill. **Status:** Common localised resident in groups or small flocks; may accompany other waxbills. **Habitat:** Dambos and other marshlands in wetter northern half of Zambia. **Voice:** Soft, high-pitched chattering.

Nigel Voaden / CC BY-SA

Casper Badenhorst

Common Waxbill
Estrilda astrild

10–13cm Sexes similar. A grey-brown waxbill with bright red bill and eye-stripe, fine dark barring on upperparts and flanks, and whitish to pale brown, buff or pink on underparts. Usually has a crimson patch on belly. Juv. has buffier underparts, narrower eye-stripe and black bill. **Status:** Common, widespread, highly gregarious resident, usually in flocks and may mix with other waxbills. **Habitat:** Rank vegetation along the edges of streams, rivers, floodplains and dambos; old cultivated fields, sometimes gardens. **Voice:** A high-pitched chittering.

Albert Froneman/Images of Africa ×2

Orange-breasted Waxbill
Amandava subflava

9cm A tiny waxbill with an orange breast patch, orange-red rump and grey-brown barring on flanks. Bill and eye-stripe are red. Female is duller with no red eye-stripe. Juv. has unbarred flanks and black bill. **Status:** Widespread resident, usually in small flocks. Uncommon at lower levels. Moves to drier grasslands in rains. **Habitat:** Moist grassland, bulrushes and rank secondary growth in dambos and floodplains. **Voice:** A series of chipping or chittering notes.

Race *O. a. muelleri* ♂

Race *O. a. muelleri* ♀

Quailfinch
Ortygospiza atricollis

9cm A tiny finch with conspicuous barring on breast and flanks; wings and rump are grey, and bill red. Race *O. a. muelleri* has white 'spectacles' and chin. Male has black forehead and throat, grey in female. Race *O. a. fuscata* lacks spectacles, and has black head, blackish-brown upperparts and chestnut breast. Juv. is paler, browner below, with black bill. **Status:** *O. a. muelleri* is a common resident in west, sparse elsewhere. *O. a. fuscata* is widespread in wetter half of Zambia. **Habitat:** Short, moist to dry grasslands. **Voice:** Harsh chittering and buzzy notes.

Bronze Mannikin
Lonchura cucullata

9cm Sexes similar. Small, abundant species with dull brown nape and back. Head, throat and upper breast are black with metallic sheen. Lower breast and belly are white, with blackish barring on flanks. Upper mandible is black, lower mandible bluish-grey. Rump also barred. Juv. has greyer upperparts, and paler throat and breast. **Status:** Widespread and gregarious throughout Zambia in small family flocks. **Habitat:** Open grassland and woodland, edges of dambos and thickets, and often in gardens. **Voice:** Quiet, high-pitched chittering.

Red-backed Mannikin
Lonchura nigriceps

10cm Sexes similar. A striking mannikin with black nape, rich red-brown back, and white barred panel on folded wing. Underparts are white with black mottling on the flanks. Bill is whitish. Juv. has brown upperparts, and off-white underparts with reddish tinge. **Status:** Resident in northern half of plateau, patchy in the east. Favours wet forest-edge ecotone in north, dispersing into miombo after breeding. **Habitat:** Riparian fringes and forest, and well-developed miombo. **Voice:** High-pitched 'sip' or 'seep' chirrups.

Sarah Solomon

Village Indigobird
Vidua chalybeata

10–11cm Brood-parasitic finch. Br. male is dark, glossy blue-black with red bill and legs. Non-br. male and female are grey-brown and streaked black and buff above, with brown and buff head stripes and pale supercilium. Belly is off-white, legs orange-pink. Juv. is similar, but browner overall with less distinctly streaked upperparts. **Status:** Common resident, parasitises Red-billed Firefinch. White-billed form possible in Livingstone region. **Habitat:** *Acacia* and other dry woodland types, edges of cultivation and suburban gardens. **Voice:** Scratchy or chattering notes with imitations of host.

Purple Indigobird — *Vidua purpurascens*

10–11cm Br. male is glossy blue-black with pale flight feathers. Bill is white, legs pinkish-white. Non-br. male and female are similar to other indigobird species, with white bill and pale pink legs. Juv. is similar to non-br. adults, but browner above with lighter streaking. **Status:** Localised resident, parasitises Jameson's Firefinch. **Habitat:** Open woodland, edges of thickets and riparian forest. **Voice:** High-pitched chattering or churring notes mixed with host mimicry.

Sarah Solomon x2

Dusky Indigobird — *Vidua funerea*

10–11cm Br. male is black with dull purple-blue wash and brown panel on folded wing. Bill is white, legs purplish-grey. Non-br. adults are buffy-brown above and paler below, with broad dark brown streaks on crown. Bill is grey-white, legs pinkish-grey. Juv. is like non-br. adults with indistinct streaking and buffy underparts. **Status:** Uncommon localised resident in wetter areas; parasitises African Firefinch. **Habitat:** Grassland with scattered bushes, woodland edges, thickets and plantations. **Voice:** High-pitched chattering notes that could be mixed with host song.

Lee Gutteridge

Pin-tailed Whydah — *Vidua macroura*

11–12cm (br. male 30–32cm) Easily identified br. male is black and white with red bill and long, floppy black tail. Non-br. male has black-and-white striped head and red bill. Br. female has dark brown and buff-striped head, and black bill; bill red when not br. Juv. is plain mouse-brown with pale cheek, whitish throat, and short stubby black, or red-and-black, bill. **Status:** Common widespread resident; parasitises Common Waxbill. **Habitat:** Open grassland and woodland habitat, and suburbia. **Voice:** High-pitched, tinny notes while displaying.

Long-tailed Paradise Whydah
Vidua paradisaea

13–14cm (br. male 36–39cm) Br. male has distinctive long, tapered tail, straw-yellow nape and pale chestnut breast. Non-br. male and female have grey upperparts with buff scaling, and a crown streaked with buff and dark grey. Cheeks have a dark C-shaped mark; bill is black. Juv. has plain grey upperparts. **Status:** Common resident in drier areas; parasitises Green-winged Pytilia. **Habitat:** Open deciduous and *Acacia* woodland, grasslands; mopane when not breeding. **Voice:** Sparrow-like chatters, trilling sounds and flute-like notes.

Broad-tailed Paradise Whydah
Vidua obtusa

13–14cm (br. male 26–28cm) A wydah with dark coppery rufous nape, deep chestnut breast and black bill. Female lacks dark C-mark on cheek. Upperparts are grey-brown with black streaks. Non-br. male and female have grey bill, and boldly streaked white and dark grey head. Juv. is like female, with plain grey-brown upperparts. **Status:** Locally common resident, prefers wetter regions. Parasitises Orange-winged Pytilia. **Habitat:** Open woodlands, generally avoids mopane. **Voice:** Twitters, cheeps; imitates host call.

Western Yellow Wagtail   *Motacilla flava*

16–17cm Sexes similar. A variable wagtail with diagnostic short tail; upperparts are olive-green and underparts yellow. Female is duller, with browner upperparts and yellow underparts fading to white on throat. Many different races occur, varying in head pattern. Juv. is similar to female, browner above. **Status:** Uncommon Palaearctic migrant from October to April. Occurs throughout the plateau in small numbers, often amongst grazing animals. **Habitat:** Short grassland in large floodplains, pastures, dambos, edges of dams. **Voice:** Shrill series of trills, but seldom calls when in Zambia.

Race *M. f. thunbergi*

Inset: Lee Gutteridge

Race *M. f. flava*

Cape Wagtail

Motacilla capensis

17–20cm Sexes similar. A greyish-brown wagtail. Zambian bird has olive-grey upperparts, a yellowish wash on white underparts, and a black breast band reduced to a small spot in centre of breast. Outer tail feathers are white. Juv. upperparts are browner, with more pronounced yellow wash below. **Status:** Uncommon localised resident; occurs in small family units, may achieve high densities in suitable feeding grounds. **Habitat:** Floodplains and edges of other wetlands. **Voice:** Song various trills and whistles.

African Pied Wagtail

Motacilla aguimp

20cm Sexes similar. A striking bird. Br. male is black and white with large, solid white patch on wing and a narrow black 'V' on the throat. Tail is black and outer tail feathers are white. Non-br. male has slate-grey upperparts. Br. female has less intense upperparts. Non-br. female has olive-grey upperparts. Juv. upperparts are grey-brown; buffy-white replaces white. **Status:** Common widespread resident, restricted to major rivers in dry west. **Habitat:** Any water's edge, suburbia, buildings and bridges. **Voice:** Song is a melodious mix of whistles and shrill notes.

Roy Glasspool

Roy Glasspool

Fülleborn's Longclaw

Macronyx fuelleborni

20cm Sexes similar. A large yellow-breasted longclaw with streaked grey-buff upperparts. A narrow black 'necklace' runs from base of bill across upper breast, becoming broader. The head and neck are grey with deep lemon-yellow supercilium. Juv. is duller overall and narrow necklace is sometimes absent. **Status:** Common localised resident with some local movement; absent from Luangwa Valley and eastern plateau. **Habitat:** Drier dambos and grassland, dam edges and marshes; scarce on major wetlands (Kafue Flats). **Voice:** Single, repetitive two-note whistle

Rosy-throated Longclaw *Macronyx ameliae*

19–20cm Sexes similar. A slender, long-tailed longclaw with diagnostic bright pink throat bordered by a black 'necklace', broadest in the centre. Pink wash on the lower breast and belly. Brown upperparts are heavily streaked black. Female is paler with a streaked, not solid, breast band. Juv. underparts are buffy, with faint pink colouring. **Status:** Uncommon localised resident. **Habitat:** Permanently or seasonally wet grassland, moist centres of dambos, and marshy areas. **Voice:** A repetitive double-note 'tee-yooo' call.

Nik Borrow

African Pipit *Anthus cinnamomeus*

16–17cm Sexes similar. Common pipit species with distinct streaking on breast, diagnostic conspicuous white outer tail feathers and yellow base to lower mandible. Makes a dipping aerial display. Juv. has dark russet upperparts, blotched breast and pinkish lower mandible. **Status:** Fairly common widespread resident in the drier areas, usually solitary. **Habitat:** Open grassland habitat, preferably short or recently burnt; edges of dambos, airfields, fallow cultivated lands and montane grassland. **Voice:** Song three to four high-pitched notes. Single 'chip' call in flight.

Derek Keats from Johannesburg, South Africa / CC BY 2.0

Wood Pipit *Anthus nyassae*

16–18cm Sexes similar. A large ground-dwelling bird with bold, dark band through eye and clear white eyebrow. Streaked above but from a distance may appear plain-backed. Breast streaks do not reach flanks. Tail is long with buff-white outer feathers. Base of bill is yellow, occasionally pinkish. Juv. is dark, with heavily spotted breast. **Status:** Fairly common localised resident. Flies into the canopy if disturbed; walks along branches. **Habitat:** Miombo woodland, also *Burkea* and open *Baikiaea* woodland. **Voice:** Song is a high-pitched series of chirps; call is a single whistle.

Grant Reed

Buffy Pipit
Anthus vaalensis

17–18.5cm Sexes similar. A large, slender pipit with plain, sandy-brown upperparts, weak breast markings and a malar stripe. Mantle is unmarked. Outer tail feathers are buff. Bill base is pink. Actively wags tail up and down, often with whole body movement. Juv. darker above with bold spotting below. **Status:** Fairly common intra-African br. migrant April to November; some birds remain year-round. **Habitat:** Short, frequently burnt grassland, well-grazed farmland, airfields and dirt roads. **Voice:** Series of sparrow-like chirps.

Plain-backed Pipit
Anthus leucophrys

16–17cm Sexes similar. A large pipit with plain, grey-brown back and indistinct breast markings. Has a pronounced white eyebrow and yellow base to the bill. Outer tail feathers are buff. Separated with difficulty from the Buffy Pipit, but does not wag tail as vigorously. Juv. has browner upperparts and more marked breast. **Status:** Widespread resident in small numbers throughout plateau. **Habitat:** Moist grassland, dambos and agricultural land. In dry season, favours burnt ground. **Voice:** Call is a low-pitched series of single or multiple trills. Does not sing during circular aerial flight.

Striped Pipit
Anthus lineiventris

17–18cm Sexes similar. A large pipit with heavily streaked breast; streaks extend to belly and flanks. Upperparts are mottled greenish-grey. Wing and tail feathers have yellow-green edges; outer tail feathers are white. Juv. upperparts are paler, lightly spotted below. **Status:** Resident, easily overlooked when not calling. Strides around rocky areas. **Habitat:** Rocky escarpments and wooded hills in miombo woodland in east of country. **Voice:** Song a loud mix of melodious notes, usually given from a perch; also a monotonous, repeated, single, deep chirping note.

Lee Gutteridge

Bushveld Pipit
Anthus caffer

13–14cm A small, boldly streaked woodland pipit with golden-brown upperparts. Large eye has white eye-ring. Breast is streaked dark brown, buff flanks also streaked. Outer tail feathers are white. Juv. is paler above. **Status:** Uncommon resident with some local movement, confined almost entirely to plateau woodlands west of Luangwa Valley. Perches quietly in trees, easily overlooked. **Habitat:** Short grass in broad-leaved woodland such as miombo. **Voice:** When flushed makes a slurred 'sweep' call.

Lee Gutteridge

Black-faced Canary
Crithagra capistrata

11–12cm Small canary with short, stubby bill. Male has extensive black mask, olive-green upperparts and yellow underparts. Female has no black on face, and light brown streaks on throat, breast and flanks. Juv. is like female but paler and more heavily streaked below. **Status:** Resident, mostly in pairs. Congregates in small post-br. flocks with local movements. **Habitat:** Edges and clearings in moist evergreen forests, thickets near dambos; occasionally well-developed miombo in high rainfall areas. **Voice:** Series of soft whistles and trills.

♂

Nik Borrow

Roy Glasspool

♀

Black-throated Canary
Crithagra atrogularis

11–12cm Sexes similar. A small, pale grey-brown canary with distinctive bright yellow rump and black tail with white tip. Black throat is diagnostic; female throat less black. Juv. has some black throat spots, and is more streaked below. **Status:** Locally common resident on Kalahari Sands in southwest and parts of the north. Occurs in pairs and small flocks, with post-br. wandering. **Habitat:** Dry, open savanna with *Acacia* thorn-scrub, miombo and *Burkea* woodland. **Voice:** High-pitched mix of soft whistles and trills.

Maans Booysen

Yellow-fronted Canary *Crithagra mozambica*

11–13cm Sexes similar but female paler. A small canary with bright yellow forehead, supercilium and cheek, and clear black malar stripe. Eye is brown; crown and nape olive-grey. Yellow rump in flight is diagnostic. Juv. is duller, with lightly streaked underparts. **Status:** Common widespread resident found singly or in pairs, forming post-br. flocks. **Habitat:** Any woodland, riparian fringing forest, cultivation and gardens. **Voice:** Various high-pitched whistles and trills.

Roy Glasspool

Brimstone Canary *Crithagra sulphurata*

13–15cm Sexes similar. A medium-sized canary with a well-developed, horn-coloured bill, greenish wash on head and upperparts, and bright yellow supercilium. Underparts vary from greenish-yellow to pale yellow. Female is slightly duller. Juv. underparts are paler and lightly streaked **Status:** Common localised resident congregating in small flocks post-br. **Habitat:** Montane grasslands and bracken–briar, open woodland and bushes, rank river vegetation, edges of cultivation and gardens. **Voice:** Song a soft trill; the call is a harsh 'trit'.

Maans Booysen

Black-eared Seedeater *Crithagra mennelli*

13–14cm Sexes similar. A grey-brown medium-sized canary with streaked black-and-white crown and white supercilium. Face is distinctively sooty black, with large pinkish-horn bill. Underparts are grey-white, with short brown streaks on breast flanks. Female crown is streaked brown, face is dark brown, and underparts are more heavily streaked. Juv. is similar to female, with browner face and more heavily streaked below. **Status:** Locally common resident. **Habitat:** Favours miombo woodland; absent from *Baikiaea* woodlands in west. **Voice:** Canary-like twitters and whistles.

Cinnamon-breasted Bunting
Emberiza tahapisi

14–15cm Sexes similar. A bunting with cinnamon-coloured body and diagnostic bold black-and-white stripes on head of male. Female duller and paler than male; crown with grey-brown, buffy facial stripes in-between white stripes. Juv. is like female with brown flecks below. **Status:** Widespread intra-African br. migrant with limited numbers remaining year-round. Post-br. dispersal into any open country. **Habitat:** Rocky, hilly country and bare stony areas. **Voice:** Soft, rather scratchy notes.

Golden-breasted Bunting
Emberiza flaviventris

15–16cm Sexes similar. A yellow-breasted bunting. Male has black head with white stripes above and below eye. Underparts are dark yellow, breast is deep golden-orange. Female is duller, with washed brown head markings and less richly coloured breast. Juv. is similar to female but duller, with streaks on breast. **Status:** Widespread common resident throughout Zambia. **Habitat:** Open woodland, also scattered trees on rocky hills. **Voice:** Various plaintive whistles.

Cabanis's Bunting
Emberiza cabanisi

16–17cm Sexes similar. A bunting with solid black cheeks. Male has bright yellow underparts, grey mantle, black cheeks and single white stripe above the eye. Female is paler and browner than male. Juv. is like female but has chestnut head, and tawny eye-stripe and wing coverts. **Status:** Resident, locally common throughout. Occasionally wanders to lower levels. **Habitat:** Mainly miombo woodland, infrequently mopane or *Acacia*. **Voice:** A series of soft, melodious whistles.

INDEX